Whirligig Beetles and Tackety Boots

by

Julia Mackenzie

Reprinted 2002, 2005, 2013

Produced by *Blaisdon Publishing*
3 Park Chase, Hornby, Bedale,
North Yorkshire DL8 1PR
www.blaisdon.f9.co.uk

This Autobiography relates to actual events and nothing is intended to vitiate, or misrepresent any real persons, alive or dead.

Proceeds from the sale of this book will go to help the work of Blythswood Care, Evanton, Ross-shire, Christian organisation for the relief of poverty

ISBN 1 90283807 6
978 190283807 6

Cover: Kyle Rona House

DEDICATED TO THE MEMORY OF MY DEAR
MOTHER AND FATHER,

JULIA AND NORMAN CUMMING

AND TO ARTHUR WHO LOVED RAASAY AS
MUCH AS I DO.

Acknowledgements

My thanks are due to many people who have helped in various ways:

To my daughter, Heather, for many hours of hard labour deciphering my handwritten scrawl, as she typed the book from my manuscript.

To Hector, my husband, for his patience and practical help.

To Rona, my daughter, for reminding me years ago that I should write for posterity about my unusual childhood and teenage years.

My sincere thanks also to relatives who contributed photographs.

My sister Peggy MacKay

My niece Janet Knowles

My niece Rebecca MacKay

Also thanks to Alison, Kenny and Marty for their help.

Foreword

I was born on 16th March 1923 on a remote island in the Inner Hebrides. Eilean Tighe (island of the house) lies off the north end of the Island of Raasay. I attended Torran School on Raasay and later Portree High School on the Isle of Skye for some time. At the age of eighteen, I joined the A.T.S., went to France and later to Germany with the 121 British General Hospital. While there, I visited the notorious Bergen Belsen concentration camp. In France, I met my future husband Arthur (George) Goffin and we married in 1947.

Widowed in 1978, I moved to Inverness where I now live with my second husband, Hector MacKenzie.

The writing of this book has fulfilled a dream I had for many years. To many today, life on our island may seem primitive, but believe me, it was a very happy, carefree life.

My daughter, Rona, prompted me to write my story; otherwise, that way of life, now completely disappeared, would be lost to future generations.

Julia Mackenzie

Cala-Na-Sìth

EILEAN TIGHE

My Dream had, after thirty years, become a reality. Here was I, once more looking at what was left of the house where I was born and where I spent the first few years of my childhood. How can I describe my feelings at that moment; the many scenes that passed before my mind's eye, one after the other, awakened from the distant past, by this visit to "Eilean Tighe" (The Island of the House). Indeed, in my young days, there was only one house on the island, my parents'. There was a ruin of another, from the past known in the Gaelic as "Tote Tigh Bellac" (the ruins of Bella's House); I never knew who Bella was.

So often I had returned to this island in my dreams – whatever the subject, the setting was usually here, or on nearby Kyle Rona, where I spent the second part of my childhood. How did I come to be here, after such a lapse of time?

Over the years, I had often planned just such a visit, but for various reasons it hadn't materialised till now. I suppose the blame could be laid at Adolf Hitler's door for starting World War Two. During those missing years, I joined the ATS, and met my late husband Arthur, an Englishman, who sadly has passed away since I first started to put my memories onto paper.

I brought up two children during that time, and although I visited my mother and father on the Island of Raasay, Eilean Tighe was too far a journey for the children. My parents had, by then, moved on to the south end of the Island of Raasay. All these things prevented me from making this much longed for visit to Eilean Tighe.

The house at Eilean Tighe was originally lived in by my maternal grandfather John Nicholson, a Gaelic bard.

When my grandmother died at quite an early age, my mother and father went to live with grandfather, Shonnie Mòr, as he was called, which translated into English means 'Big John', and he certainly was a big strong man. But more about him later. When I was about nine years old, my parents moved to the main Island of Raasay – to a place called Kyle Rona, about two miles across from the tidal island of Eilean Tighe, where my father was a postman to the lighthouse on the island of Rona. At sometime during the war years, after my father had retired, they moved to the south end of Raasay.

This year, I decided this yearning must be satisfied. Maybe, I was spurred on by the realisation that the very long arduous walk to reach my destination would, in a few years time, become an impossibility for ageing bones – and how could I live with my unfulfilled dream?

So, it was that I persuaded Arthur and my brother John to make this sentimental journey with me. We emerged from John's house at 6a.m. on the first leg of our journey.

John had voluntarily taken on the burden of carrying our coffee flasks and sandwiches, no doubt knowing we would find the trek gruelling enough without any extra weight. John was used to the rough roads and hills, as he often had to traverse them after his sheep. What a beautiful morning it was; everywhere was very still, only the call of a seabird here and there to break the silence as we left Inverarish on the first part of the journey by car to Brochel Castle. In my young days, this was a hamlet with two families living there – there is also a ruined castle. I believe it was built to keep the Mackenzies of Gairloch from invading Raasay. The Piermaster on Raasay at this time was Peter Gillies, who took us as far as we could get by car. From here on, we were dependant on 'Shank's Pony'. Before setting off on our long walk, we arranged for Peter to pick us up that evening at about 6.30 p.m. to take us back to Inverarish where John lived.

We stood for quite a while there at Brochel, just drinking in the beauty of the scene before us. The bay was calm and still – its beauty was breathtaking, but the Crofter's houses, which had both been occupied in my school days looked forlorn and unhappy, as did the old castle itself, perched on its natural rock foundation. As I gazed at the old grey castle, I thought of what tales it could tell of days past. One of the houses was a complete ruin, but the other was in the process of being restored – I understood, by an English gentleman. I envied the absent 'Sassenach' for the view he would have from his window – the beautiful bay and across the sea to the hills of Applecross.

In memory, I was taken back to my school days, when the Grahams and Mackenzies lived in these two houses and worked the crofts. I recalled the fabulous openhearted welcome all travellers received from these kind folks. I just had to walk down the overgrown path to the houses and, looking through the window of the now modernised Mrs. Mackenzie's house, I was amazed to see the latest in kitchen units and other equipment. My first thought was, "What would the old lady, Mrs Mackenzie, have said to all that" – I could almost hear her voice, "Ach iad fhèin s'an gadgets" – ('Ach themselves and their gadgets'). I don't think she would have much time for these new-fangled things. I remembered with a touch of sadness, the happy folk who used to live here; I'm quite sure they hadn't much of this world's goods, but they were contented. We would have liked to linger here in this peaceful setting, but time would not allow us, so we had to be on our way.

We covered the next three miles (Highland miles, I believe) in good time, stopping now and again to admire the sheer beauty of the everlasting hills around us. The sea was calm and blue and, as the road, in places, dropped down near enough, we could see rocks and seaweed and even fish swimming around. While across the water, the hills of Skye made a truly panoramic scene. I have always told friends in England eager to see Skye, that the best way to view it is to visit Raasay and look over at Skye from there. My husband put it all in a nutshell, when he exclaimed, "Who wants foreign holidays when we have all this on our doorstep."

I cannot pass from here without a mention of this road from Brochel to the next hamlet of Arnish. This road was the self-imposed Herculean task of one man, a cousin of mine, Calum MacLeod. He made the road single-handed and it took him ten years. One has to see it to understand the perseverance and hard work it entailed. Calum and his wife were the last remaining inhabitants of this end of Raasay. Sadly, Calum has passed away since I started to write this; he was a wonderful man with a brilliant brain.

TORRAN

Our next stop was the hamlet of Torran just beyond Arnish. We had decided not to call at Arnish just now, as we had met Calum and he had invited us to have tea with them on the way back. In my school days, Torran had a school, schoolteacher's house, a church and three occupied houses. The schoolhouse was still in very good order, as was the nearby church. We entered the now gateless and overgrown school playground.

It didn't take much imagination to hear children's Gaelic voices; I was reminded of the games we used to play on the nearby flat piece of ground – '*Stealing the Crown'* was the favourite. There were two teams and the crown was usually a stick and held by one side to start. The other side had to steal it without being caught by one of the opposing side. If you were caught, you had to stand still where you were, unless one of your team could come and tap you, then you were free to join in the game once more. The game finished when one side stole the crown and didn't have any of their team left as prisoners with the other side. I remember it being great fun for most of us, but after a lot of rain, it became very muddy.

On one occasion, I recall a friend, Chrissie Graham (one of the Brochel Castle Grahams) falling in the mud and getting a severe telling off from her older sister, Mary, who I suppose was keeping an eye on her.

Sitting on the step of one of the school porches, John and I did a lot of reminiscing, as we refreshed ourselves with coffee and sandwiches. These porches were our cloakrooms, and one was for boys and one for girls, although as far as my memory goes, in my day, there were never more than 10 or 12 pupils. I recall sitting on these same steps on my first day at school along with my sister, Betty. I also remember how one of the boys, Charlie Mackenzie, also from Brochel, frightened us by taking out a penknife and saying he was going to cut off our toes. It was genuine fear as we were barefooted, (we saved our boots for the winter), was it really so long ago?

Looking out in front of the school was beautiful Torran Bay, like a mirror reflecting the heather clad hills around it. I felt it was such a waste that there was so few to admire it. Surely, such beauty was not created to be left unloved and unviewed. At the back of the school, there before us were the same hazel trees from which, in our playtime, we gathered nuts to take home and store for Halloween, when dooking for nuts was the highlight of the night. Mother would get the old galvanized bath out, fill it with water and we would take turns in dooking for nuts – it was good fun until one of the others pushed your head into the water. If we were fortunate enough and father had been to the shop in nearby Skye, we may have had false faces. One year, I recall, I cut out one from the (now gone forever) *People's Journal.* It was a Santa Claus one. I had to cut it out and paint it; it looked very good, with a bit of elastic to tie it on. John and I located the well of cool clear water near the school. This well had often refreshed our bodies and, I think, our minds as well, for many times it broke the monotony of lessons. The procedure was this, you would put up your hand to draw teachers attention and say, "Please Miss may I get out", it could be either for a drink of water or for a more urgent bodily call. We didn't always go to the well, or if we did, it was a mere formality. I have wondered since how the teacher did not cotton on.

But I must hurry on; the next call was to the old church nearby and, as we peered through the windows, I seemed again to hear the beautiful Gaelic psalm singing, with our father's voice presenting, or as they say in the Gaelic, 'cur a-mach na lòidne'. There was no music, but they didn't really need it. I have wondered many a time since, how these men learned the tunes, as none of them had tune books, and if they had, they couldn't read them. Then, one of the Godly men of old would read and expound the gospel to the little flock. It was quite hard to bring myself back to the present and realise it was all in the past; but at that moment, it came to me how thankful was their sincerity and reverence for the things of God. It was their example that brought me in later years to a personal faith in Jesus Christ as my Saviour.

* * *

The road to Kyle Rona lies ahead of us now with all its schoolday memories. We used to walk the four miles to school over rough sheep tracks, for you couldn't call it a road. When my sister Betty and I started school, because of the distance, we were allowed one day off a week. It's a far cry from the beautiful bicycles and handy school transport of today, but I'm quite convinced that the children today are not as happy as we were, even with all the T.V.s, etc. Our T.V. was everywhere. Along the road, we came across all kinds of wonderful things, tadpoles in the pools and plenty of toads and frogs. What a thrill it was to find a peat bog with plenty of frogs' spawn, lift it and let it slither through your fingers. Then to watch each day the tadpoles arrive, and then the baby frogs. Then there were these strange insects, the 'water boatmen' skating across the water, and those dizzy 'whirly beetles' with their never-ending twirling dance. Children today are missing an awful lot; TV and lots of pocket money can never make up for seeing nature as it is with your own eyes. I don't think my grandchildren will have such lovely memories as I have of my childhood.

With rabbits and hares scampering about, we were really excited when we found a bird's nest. We looked each week till the chicks hatched. I remember once finding a bird's nest with five beautiful, bluey-grey eggs in it. Then, when we looked one day, there were six and the new egg was larger than the others. Of course, we realised that this was a cuckoo's egg. So, it was that, one by one, the other eggs were pushed out, and then this huge greedy chick took over and the poor little sparrow had her work cut out feeding it. So, we gave a hand by finding some worms and dropping then into the mouth of the interloper. If it wasn't for its very welcome call in the Spring, I wouldn't like the cuckoo at all.

This road from Torran to Kyle Rona is now overgrown with rushes and, in places, the heather has taken over, but not really that much worse than in my young days. Here and there I could even remember certain stones sticking out of the path – that were a painful memory – remember, we walked to school barefooted when the weather was warm enough, and these very stones were the ones where my poor toes had suffered the most, as I stubbed my feet against them. In winter, we wore boys' 'tackety boots', with steel plates on toes and heels. They were the only footwear suitable and lasting. They were called 'tackety boots' because of the steel studs in the soles, the tackets.

Something else that came to my mind very forcibly was the hunger pangs, as we made our long trek home. There were no school dinners then, although our teacher's Auntie, who was called Alice MacDonald, helped a lot in the dinnertime, by giving us hot cocoa to drink that helped our 'piece and jam' to go down. We sometimes also had with us a piece of oatcake with evil smelling salted highland butter on it (and even now I can't bear salted butter), but it was very welcome after school or at dinner time – to 'keep the wolf from the door'.

Let me explain about the 'salt butter'. It would have been made at home months before, and put in a crock with a lid on to keep and mature, and it certainly matured. Many times, we were so hungry that we used to turn out our school satchels in case there were crumbs lurking at the bottom, or maybe in our coat pockets. It reminds me of the day when someone else had looked for crumbs in my pocket. I had just climbed the little hill path above the school, when I felt a queer flutter inside my coat. I flung my coat off, and Betty and I had a hilarious time guiding a mouse out of the lining of my coat. What a happy time we had, free as the air, among nature and its natural surprises.

As we walked along the old path, with a memory in each bend, I looked for old Mrs. Nicolson's house down below the road in a hollow under the hill. I couldn't see it at all and then John reminded me that there were only the walls left now. How very sad – I could remember it as a picturesque thatched house. I called the lady of the house 'old Mrs. Nicolson' just now, but really, she wasn't old at all, just appeared old to us children, as she was my mother's contemporary. How often I had seen 'Nannag' as she was fondly called, standing at her door and shouting at the top of her voice to make us children hear. We always knew then that she had some message for my mother – come to think of it, she must have had a powerful voice, as her house was quite a distance from the road. Sometimes, she would leave a bottle of milk by the roadside for us if our cows had gone dry, and we returned the favour if similar circumstances befell her family. Now the place is quiet and still and everywhere has a mournful look.

We come to more well-remembered scenes, but here is a special place where I had to stop – at a well of clear spring water – I wanted to taste it again. In my school days, it was always kept clean, with a jam jar nearby as a drinking vessel. But alas, it is now undrinkable and looked stagnant; no one uses it now, just another sad reminder of the passing of time.

We had quite a steep climb now till we came to 'Faireadh an dà mhuir' – Gaelic for the 'view of the two seas'. That name is very descriptive. As we reached the top, we sat down to rest awhile and to drink in the splendour of the view before us. From one side, one looked across the outer Sound of Raasay to Applecross, and on the other the Inner Sound across the sea to the Cullin Hills of Skye. Now we are going downhill to 'Beallach a' chruidh' – the cattle gap – a very steep descent indeed. I am reminded of the many times we did a bit of rock climbing, I wonder what excuse we gave for being late home; which reminds me that there were times that we didn't need an excuse, we had a good one in the shape of my father's highland bull. This animal would suddenly appear on the top of a hill, bellowing and pawing the ground. What detours we made to hide from him! It was very frightening, as he seemed to try and catch up with us because, as we ran, he appeared on a nearer hill and you could hear him for miles. It left me with a terror of bulls of any description. I think if he appeared now, I wouldn't even think of running, I'd be rooted to the spot. He was, of course, very dangerous, as will be seen from the fact that he had to be shot as he turned on my father. I actually seem to remember that his time had run out anyway, and that was why a man with a shotgun was at hand.

Now we walk a bit further and we come to a place called in the Gaelic 'glac tobar Catriona' – the valley of Catriona's well. We were very frightened when going through this dismal gap, more so in the dim winter evenings. Remember that, although our days up here are longer in the summer, the nights come in earlier and so most winter nights it would be dusk coming home from school. The reason for our fear of this place, was that many times we had heard our elders discussing how it was haunted by the ghost of a man who stole some tools while helping to make the so-called road walkable. The story goes like this:

He hid the tools under a large boulder (still there) and, unfortunately for him, he died before he could retrieve them. For a long time afterwards, his ghost was seen sitting on this boulder, and according to folk who were living at the time, was seen by people who knew him. Someone must have been curious enough to investigate and found the tools. Once they were removed, the apparition disappeared.

We now emerge from this spooky place and walk along to the Kyle Rona sheep fanks. Here, I have only pleasant memories of sheep shearing and peat cutting. Peat cutting was a lovely time, when very often we would light a fire and cook our dinner – usually potatoes and salt herring, then go to some nearby source of fresh water, fill the kettle and when it boiled, just put the tea in – best cup of tea you ever tasted. Maybe it had something to do with the peaty water – after all it's good for whisky making.

We would all sit down on the grass or heather and enjoy mother's fresh baked girdle scones and oatcakes. What a feast, and in such surroundings! Over to my right, I can still make out the deep cuts on the ground where father cut the peat. These cuts are called peat bogs and, when they filled with water when the rain came, they made excellent places for sailing our homemade wooden boats. Father was very clever at making these. I recall a really fine one he made for me once, hollowed out and with wooden seats. It also had a mast and mother helped make a sail for it. My – it could travel when a great gust of wind caught it. It didn't seem strange to me that a small girl should be sailing boats, instead of playing with dolls, but dolls were such a luxury. Sometimes, a relation would come home from Glasgow, most usually either our Auntie Mary Forbes or one of her family; they would bring a present of a doll or some other toy. I especially remember one such doll; she came in a lovely presentation box with paper lace round the edges and the doll tied to the inside of the box with elastic. She had beautiful hair and eyes that moved and closed when she was laid down. She also had removable shoes, but she was too precious to be played with. She was put up, in her box on the wooden shelf above the dresser, just to be admired. I can't remember how long she was kept there, but I suppose, eventually, she was brought down to be played with.

Of course, boats were the big thing in our lives, as we could every day watch drifters and trawlers and various other craft going up and down to and from the 'Minch'. But, back to the 'Peat Cutting'. This task was usually performed during the summer holidays. The procedure was that father would first clear the top layer of grass and heather off the top of the peat bog. This was done with a very broad spade called a 'caibe làir', and then he would press a special peat-cutting instrument (iarunn mòine) into the ground. Up would come a beautiful black shiny oblong of peat, just like a large lump of liquorice. The peat iron was shaped in such a way as to cut it in this handy shape. We children would stand in a convenient position, with arms outstretched to catch the lump of peat as father aimed it our way. After a while, one became expert at timing every thrust of the peat iron and the exact moment when a lovely wet slippery peat would land on your outstretched hands. Next, this peat was laid down in rows on the grassy ground beside us, to await the next stage of peat making, which was called 'rùghan'. It just meant tiny wigwams of four peat lumps stood on end and one across the top, to finish the sun drying process. The final stage was gathering all the peat into one big heap called a 'Cruach'. It was given its final ornamental and rain protective finish by peat being laid end on and overlapping. This type of finish kept the rain from soaking into the peat inside. The whole thing when it was finished looked like a door-less, windowless house, and very ornamental.

While at this place, we also looked at the old sheep fank, where the men would pen the sheep for shearing. It was just a pen made like a dry-stone dyke. No electric shears in those days – usually some of the men from the neighbouring island of Fladda would come and help. One of them I especially remember, for the speed with which he completed the task. His name was Callum MacLeod, but to distinguish him from many Callum MacLeods in Raasay, I will give his usual name, which was Callum Beag. I suppose this made it easier for his mother to call the right Callum, as his father was called Callum Mòr (Beag is small and Mòr is big). At this sheep-shearing time, all the family would help and as always, mother was there with the food. What a wonderful happy time it was. We have spent more time at the Kyle Rona fank than we intended, but it was so nice to relive these memories of scenes gone forever now. With all the new technology, there doesn't seem to be any time to enjoy what they are doing nowadays. It all seems so far removed from our happy family get-togethers.

As we journeyed on, we come to 'Lochan a ghrùgaich'. I am not sure of the meaning of the last word, but I was told years ago it referred to the leeches which lived in this loch – lochan, of course just means a small lake. One end of the loch was quite shallow and was used by mother as a laundrette. She would light a fire between the large stones over which father had placed a huge iron boiler. At the edge of the loch was a nice flat stone on which she beat the clothes with a wooden club to get them clean. Finally, after a rinse in the lovely soft water, it was laid out on the hillside to bleach in the sun. During the school holidays, when we were old enough, Betty and I would do our own washing there; it was great fun. After our washing was done, we paddled in the loch, but not for long, for the leeches would come and stick themselves onto our legs. I wasn't very fond of them; they had suction pads at one end and were black and slimy. They also seemed to be able to expand and contract at will. I didn't know what they were then, but now I believe they were leeches and if I am wrong, perhaps some reader would correct me. One had to give quite a tug to get them to release their grip. We never went near the other end of the loch that was said to be bottomless and haunted as well; maybe the ghost story was invented to keep children away from this dangerous place. It was said that a child's ghost could sometimes be seen. The child was supposed to have drowned there a long time ago. These ghostly tales made us hurry past such places when coming home from school, and this was certainly a most eerie place in the dusk. I recall one special evening Betty and I were just coming past the loch when we heard the most awful groaning. Of course, we took to our heels, but the groans seemed to follow us, and I can vividly remember Betty tripping up over a tuft of rushes in the middle of the path. It was only then the ghost revealed himself in the person of my brother John, who even now is full of those kinds of tricks.

DOIRE DUBH meaning 'Black Dell'

Near Kyle Rona are the ruins of another small township called Doire Dubh. There, you can see the stonewalls of what were once the homes of the older generation. One of the ruins is of my paternal grandfather's home. His name was Murdo Cumming. His father had come as a herdsman to the tidal Island of Fladda to the north west of Raasay. His son married a Peggy MacLeod from Arnish; they lived in Doire Dubh and had eight in their family. My father stayed at home when their mother died, and worked the Croft and looked after the younger ones; the rest went away to work. Looking at the ruin of the house, one wonders how they all managed for sleeping. I don't really know much about my Cumming grandparents, as they both died before I was born.

Away to the right is an amazing modern looking shell of a house. It was built by a man, Alasdair Gillies, locally known as Sùlag. While he was building this house, or folly, I should say, his family lived in the house next to my father's family. I don't know what possessed him to build a house in such a place. It is perched on the edge of a sheer drop. As far as I know, he never had any building training, but the house is perfect. The stone for it was brought from quite a distance by boat, and chiselled by him to give a beautiful sculptured surface. I believe the rock was sandstone, which would lend itself to that kind of work. When we lived in Kyle Rona and used to herd the cows over at Doire Dubh, we came across heaps of asbestos roofing slates, buried deep in the bracken that, by now, had taken over. Two questions, which I've never really got an answer to: Why did Sùlag stop building when he had done so much work – he was up to roof level. Seemingly, he decided to move to the south end of Raasay, but why?

My sister Peggy told me quite a lot about Doire Dubh, as she and John were born there. She told me a really hilarious story about herself and John, and Sùlag's adopted daughter who was nicknamed 'Dempsey' – I believe after the boxer, Jack Dempsey. She seems to have been a tough big girl from all accounts. This happened on a Sunday, when no-one was supposed to go visiting, but Dempsey whose real name was Kirsty, decided she was going over to see her playmates, Peggy and John. She thought no-one had seen her, but Sùlag did, because he came after her. When he called her, she got such a fright, she took to her heels out the door and failed to see the pot of salt herring my mother had stood behind the door, ready for dinner. Dempsey caught her foot in the handle and the herring went slithering along the floor and some out the door. To save her and themselves from a severe scolding, Peggy and John never said a word to mother, but picked up the herring and put them back in the pot. The floor was earthen, so I'm sure the herring wouldn't have been too clean, but it seems they got away with it. Peggy also related to me about the time when mother went out for 'peats' and she and John were left to keep an eye on baby, Chrissie. They could gently rock her to sleep. She was in the cradle used for all of us; a beautiful handmade wooden one with a wooden bow canopy and rockers. They rocked the baby so vigorously, they rocked her out of the cradle. In those days, babies' bottles were not the sophisticated things you see today. They were round and flat with a long rubber tube that went inside, with a teat on the other end. Mother used to give Chrissie her bottle and when Peggy and John got a chance, they had quite a few drinks of it. It would be very sweet, as mothers didn't know at that time that too much sugar was bad for babies. I don't know how Chrissie survived at all, but I can assure you she did and grew up a very healthy person. She served in the W.A.A.F. during the last war, and subsequently married Sùlag's grandson

Alasdair, a farmer. To be a farmer's wife, you have to be tough, so maybe less sweet milk was good for her.

After a short walk we descend Beallach an Achaidh and there is Achadh House, Kyle Rona, the scene of many of my childhood years.

KYLE RONA

What desolation meets my eyes. The old house is still standing; its corrugated iron roof red with the rust of years, while nearby, there are sheep fanks put up by the man who has the lease of this part of the Island. We decided to have some refreshments at this house that held so many memories of my father and mother. We opened the door, which was just tied loosely with a piece of string, but once inside, I wished I had not come in at all. For here, the desolation was complete. What used to be my mothers kitchen-cum-sitting room-cum-dining room, was piled high with bags of wool. Obviously, this is where John Gillies, the sheep owner, stored the wool after shearing. Everywhere smelt strongly of sheep and I felt at that moment that, to have found the old home as just a ruin, would have been preferable. At least then, it would have retained its dignity. We pushed our way past the bags of wool into the end room, once our best bedroom, now used by the shepherds as sleeping quarters and dining room during shearing and dipping time. Here was a table and chairs and a *Calor* gas ring, plus teapot and kettle. The thought of a nice cup of tea seemed very exciting at that moment, and another drink of coffee from the flask, was not very tempting. If only we had some tea, and then my eye caught sight of what looked like a tea caddy on a nearby shelf. On opening it, I found the shepherds had really left some tea. Now to find the old well from which so long ago our family had drawn the daily quota of water – on Saturday, a double quota as no water was carried in on the 'Lord's Day' – Sunday. I found it clean and well cared for by the shepherds and, with the help of John and Arthur, I soon had a really welcome pot of tea brewing.

After this refreshing drink, I decided to have a look around all the old familiar landmarks; it was all so quiet, so beautiful and yet so very, very lonely. I felt I would have liked to hold the whole place in my arms to comfort it, if it were possible. There to my left was the old byre, and I could almost see my dear mother with the two pails of frothy milk, walking towards the house, usually with a cat in tow. Dandy, my favourite cat, had already had a squirt of milk as mother milked. He always sat waiting within squirting distance, either he was a swift mover, or my mother had a very good aim.

Back at the house, my father came vividly to my mind, as I stood on the spot where he used to gut and clean the fish after a night's fishing. He was an expert fisherman, but never used anything like the modern fishing rod and tackle; all he had was a long bamboo cane with a line and hook attached. Usually, the fly was a bit of sheep's wool, and occasionally, he used what he called a spinner – a rubber lure with a revolving wing on the end. I think these were used to catch the bigger fish, like cod and lythe. He did a lot of his fishing standing on a suitable rock and never came home empty-handed, a blessing for us too, as our main diet was fish and potatoes. Sometimes, one of my sisters, or John, or I would go out with him in the rowing boat. This was really exciting. At times, we used the rods in the boat and I wasn't very keen on that, as they were awkward to handle, especially when you tried to land a fish. Very often, we fished with the 'big line' or 'beart mhòr', which consisted of a square frame over which a strong fishing twine was wound, on the end of which was a lead weight, then a spinner and hook. This was my favourite mode of fishing, because we caught such a lot. The only time father used bait was 'cuddy fishing'. Cuddies were young coleys and at times, they used to come near the shore in shoals. At these times, he would go down to the shore and prise limpets off the rocks (we sometimes helped in this), then take them home and pour boiling water over them. This had the effect of making them fall out of their shells. Sounds cruel now, but we had to eat, and fish being our main food, this was the only way to get enough to feed us all. There were eight of us, nine when my half-brother James came home from sea. When evening came, father would go down to the shore and stand on a suitable rock, drop a handful of limpets in, and the hungry cuddies came swarming in for a feed. But, he was ready for them with his net, called a 'Tabh' in Gaelic. It was something like a huge butterfly net with a long handle. When it came up, it was crammed full of wriggling fish. I have a good memory of this operation, as sometimes, I accompanied him and fed the cuddies for him with the limpets.

But the most exciting fishing was when we went out in the evening to set some nets, rowed away to a suitable site, landed and tied the boat up, them lit a fire and, with an old kettle, made tea and ate some of mother's very tasty girdle scones and oatcakes. It was an eerie kind of scene with the moon shining on the water and, in the darkness around us, the sea showing phosphorescent lights as it lapped against the rocks. In the morning light, the nets were lifted and we rowed for home with a few weeks' supply in the boat.

At this point, you may ask, "How did we manage to keep all the fish fresh for future eating"?

Well, here is how we did it: Some were used fresh,

fried or boiled; most were salted down for eating in the winter. A lot of the fish were hung out to dry in the sun. It was the usual thing to festoon them on a line hung from one end of the house to the other and it was quite a job at times to keep the seagulls from taking their share. It must have been a very healthy way of life, as the only time I can recollect seeing a doctor there was when we were all vaccinated against smallpox. I believe it was compulsory in those days. We used age-old remedies, such as seal oil rendered down by my father and bottled – great for chestiness or sore throats. But oh, what a taste! It was so fishy. We also had our own store of cod liver oil; none of this refined stuff you get from the chemist. Father fried cod livers and then bottled the oil – it was a most unpalatable medicine, even more fishy than the seal oil, but it worked for colds and flu. It was also used for healing sprains, and the seal oil especially used on a piece of flannel and put on your chest for bronchial trouble. However, my old grandfather (more about him later) had a very special remedy for colds. It consisted of a spoonful of oatmeal mixed to a paste with whisky. I think grandfather seemed to get more colds than anyone else in the family, or least he said he had a cold!

Before we journeyed on to Eilean Tighe, I just had to get to the top of a hillock at the end of the house, here in

Kyle Rona. What memories came flooding in? How often in the early War years, I had stood here on a dark winter's night, listening to the engine noises of the ships of war, stealthily making their way up to the naval bases at Kyle of Lochalsh or Balmacara – or late on a summer's evening, watching their grey shadows, often a whole convoy and usually with a minesweeper ahead of them. I can still recall the sense of pride and security I felt at the sight of these guardians of the Nation. As I shut my eyes, I can easily hear their engines now; it doesn't seem so long ago.

As I stood there, I also remembered how my sister Betty and I had the job on summer evenings of herding the cows. That meant to watch them feeding everywhere around, except the newly shooting corn, or the potatoes now sprouting. What a chore that was, as we had to take our school homework with us, try doing long divisions and geometry, etc., with one eye on the brown cow who loved new corn and was determined to have some. At the end of the evening, the cows were put into an enclosure for the night, and then mother would come and milk them 'in situ'. It was great to see those pails of milk covered in milky froth. Betty and I had a treat, as mother filled one pail and laid it aside. We would use our fingers to scoop the lovely warm froth – no word of pasteurising then. Mother must have been a very strong woman; she often carried two pails full of milk, sometimes a couple of miles. It didn't seem to do her any harm, as she lived till she was 84 and was active in mind and body right up to the end. Her life was very hard; she brought up a large family on very little and I never heard her complain of her lot, although my third brother was a spastic child and could do nothing for himself. She carried him on her back while working out in the field at springtime and harvest. He died, I believe, at the age of fourteen, but before he died, she had the added burden of a 'Downs Syndrome' child, my youngest sister. What a happy person this wee girl was; she brought a lot of happiness into our family. We all loved her and she gave a lot of love in return.

A most exciting time in our young lives was when cousins from Glasgow came home on holiday. A special one was Cousin Angus, the youngest son of my Auntie Mary. Angus was at college in Glasgow and spent every holiday with us. He taught Betty and I some English songs and also some French ones. A favourite English one was called 'Frankie and Johnny'. Most evenings, Angus gave Betty and me some foot training. It went like this. When there was a heavy dew, he made us wash our feet in the dewy grass (remember, we never wore shoes in the summer). Then he would inspect them and, if they were not as clean as he wanted, he pretended to be severe. Off would come one of his plimsolls and we got a gentle smack. I remember he called us 'his slaves', because if he asked us to do something with one voice, we would say, "We are not your slaves." It was all good-natured fun and we were all very fond of Angus. Especially, as each year, he brought Betty and me a new dress, usually pretty floral ones, something that mother could not afford. I think probably Auntie Mary would have got them for him, as they always fitted perfectly. It was very exciting and a far cry from the demands of little girls today, who must have the latest fashions. One year, Angus brought home some of his student friends. If my memory is correct, there were three of them and they set up their tent in Doire Dùbh. Betty and I had the job of keeping them supplied with mother's baking and anything else they needed. I think they must have been heavy smokers, as they used to give us the empty cigarette boxes. We thought these were great treasures; they were the large flat tins, yellow with *Gold Flake* written on the lid. They were great for holding crayons and pencils and, of course, cigarette cards. I believe these tins held 100 cigarettes.

On winter nights, we sometimes had visitors from the sea, usually from the south end of Raasay, either lobster fishermen or maybe herring fishermen. I remember the boat was called the '*Frigate Bird*'. I think it belonged to a relation of my mother's, Calum Nicholson, or to give him his Gaelic title Calum Iain Bhig (son of little Malcolm). The crew as I recall, were my uncle, James Nicolson (Seumas Mòr), son of grandfather Shonnie Mòr, his son Ian and Calum Iain Bhig's son, Ian Mòr. They usually came ashore and had supper with us. While the older folk yarned, the two Ians taught us to play *Ludo*. We had never heard of the game, let alone played it. They brought the board with them. What fun we had and the fun was increased when our older brother James came home from a trip at sea and bought a gramophone and a couple of records. If my memory serves me correctly, he sent away for it by mail order. The records came as a package with it. They were quite odd to play in our house, as the only songs we knew were Gaelic songs, and here was something nearly foreign to us. One record was called '*Painting the Clouds with Sunshine*', and the other was the Story of Aladdin in the form of a song. I still remember the first few words, "It happened in Monterey, one night long ago." We must have played them over and over, because of the novelty of a voice coming out of this thing. It was a little black wind-up portable gramophone. Later on, James bought a more suitable record; it was Archie Grant, that fine Gaelic singer.

What a time we had with our *Ludo* and Archie Grant.

At one time in Kyle Rona, I had a spell of pigeon breeding. A cousin from the south end brought me two pigeons, a male and female. They were lovely, pure white fantails. In due course, Josephine, that's what I called her, produced two eggs and sat on them. Joseph, her husband, was very attentive looking after her. One day, what excitement, the chicks hatched out – quite ugly I thought at first, but I was fascinated with the way Josephine regurgitated the food for them. I didn't know about this, so it was quite an eye opener. Once, Josephine got broody and she hadn't laid any eggs, so I gave her a hen's egg to keep her happy and she faithfully sat on it. What a surprise for me and I'm sure mind-boggling for Josephine, the chicken hatched out and Josephine fed it as if it was her own kind. When he was big enough and able to eat chicken food, I got her out of the nest (it was a pullet). It was a bit sad to see her efforts of flight, but Josephine like a good mother, spent a lot of time on the ground with her strange daughter. Eventually, the pullet realised there were others like her and she would occasionally join the hens. She became a good layer too; my mother always called her the 'Cearc a chalmain', the 'pigeon's hen'. Unfortunately, after I left home, the pigeons began to fly further afield, probably missed me talking to them. Josephine flew as far as the Isle of Fladda and was shot by one of the men there – maybe thinking it was a wild one. Afterwards, I believe Joseph either pined away, or just disappeared.

KYLE RONA – 1939-1945 WAR

The beginning of the War seemed quite exciting for us, when everyone was told to 'blackout' their windows. We had quite a problem with ours, as our bedroom windows were what were known as 'skylights'. Very difficult, or just about impossible to curtain with blackout material, so what better than pasting layers and layers of newspapers over the windows. Very effective, but unfortunately, our bedrooms remained 'blacked out' for the duration of the War!

An exciting incident happened one day. A huge barrage balloon floated over Kyle Rona, trailing some cables. It must have broken loose from some protection area; I have often wondered where it eventually got to. It was a strange sight to see floating over our quiet little corner. It was about this time we had an unusual visitor arrive in Kyle Rona. Actually, it was 'visitors', as three arrived at first. I can still remember their names; one was Joseph Ulrich, who said he was a German Jew, Richard Candling who told us he was from the Channel Isles and

John Tonge. The other two just visited the Island of Rona with John Tonge. They asked father to ferry them across which he did. The other two did not stay long, but John Tonge did. He stayed many months in the old schoolhouse, which by then was not very habitable. Father, being the postman to Rona also delivered mail for John Tonge, many of his letters were addressed to John Von Tonge. This accounted for the rumours that circulated about him, that he was a German spy. But I would have thought that the 'Von' would have been a sure give away. But he certainly did some strange things. He never left the Island by the usual route through Raasay and then by Mail Steamer to Kyle of Lochalsh, where you had to show your certificate of residence in a 'Protected Area', which he didn't have. He usually left by hailing a fishing boat at the back of Rona. Of course, Rona would certainly have been the ideal place for spying on the British Navy, as so many warships passed that way to enter the naval bases at Kyle of Lochalsh and Balmacara. The large naval base at Loch Ewe was also near Rona, just across the water.

One day, John Von Tonge disappeared; he left his belongings behind and even food on the table. After a few months, father got worried as winter was coming on and the place was not very watertight. So, we wrote to an address that he gave us, supposing to be his mother's. We told her the condition of the place and how his possessions were being spoiled with the damp, but never a word did we get back, and John Von Tonge never returned – without a doubt a strange happening.

I was suddenly roused from my reverie by Arthur calling that the tide was now going out and it would be possible to cross to Eilean Tighe, our destination. The road from Kyle Rona to the Raasay side of the 'Caolas', meaning the 'Kyle' or 'narrow sea', which separates Raasay from Eilean Tighe, had become very overgrown with brambles, rushes and bracken. I followed it more by instinct than sight; every twist and bend brought back from the recesses of my mind. I felt happy and pleased that it had been stored in my memory. It was about a mile walk to the 'Caolas' and halfway there, looking to my right, I could see the ruins of Norman Mackenzie's house. Norman and his sister Kate lived here in my young days. When Kate died, Norman was left alone and I can remember at times, having to go to his house from Achadh house in Kyle Rona to write letters to relations of his, or to write out orders for a chemist in Kyle of Lochalsh. When I think of it now, I don't know how I kept a straight face, as his names for some of the items were quite weird. He used to call '*Carnation Milk*' in

Gaelic 'Bainne Na Bò Nach eil Ann', which translated means 'milk from the cow that doesn't exist'. I'm not sure whether he was illiterate or not, but he certainly could not write a letter, and I don't think I ever heard him speak in English. He must have been a strong pipe smoker, for when his usual quota of tobacco (*XXX Bogie Roll*) didn't arrive on time, he could be seen and heard shouting and singing (if you could call it that) Gaelic songs or even psalms. He must have been suffering withdrawal symptoms, although in those days we didn't call it that.

Now there was Norman's old home, deserted and broken down and, as I believed then, never again to hear human voices in its rooms. But since I started writing this, (it has taken many years), Norman's house has been beautifully rebuilt and is used as a walkers' 'bothy'.

As we walked to Eilean Tighe, my brother John and I recalled how, as children, after walking the long rough road from Torran school, sometimes wet, cold and hungry, we had to wait at the Caolas if the tide was in and just shout as loud as we could till either my grandfather or father heard us and pushed out the wee rowing boat to ferry us across. I believe the boat was given to my father by the education authorities for that purpose. In the morning, we had to be ferried to the other side if the tide was in, to walk all those miles to school again.

Now more about our shouting match at the Caolas. When my grandfather was alive, he had a special 'lookout' under the Rowan tree on the hill above the Caolas. If my memory serves me correctly, I think it was called 'Cnoc Na Gaoithe' – 'Windy Hill'. I could see it from where I was standing now, and I could just picture 'Shonnie Mòr' sitting there, usually whittling a piece of Alder branch, which he made into fantastic whistles for our amusement. He was a fine old gentleman and a Gaelic Bard. I am sure a lot of his beautiful Gaelic songs were composed sitting under that very tree. His songs were composed from the heart, 'of old, unhappy, far off things and battles long ago', but also, at times, very amusing ones, such as one composed about a man building a house on the nearby Isle of Rona. Seemingly, there had been a lot of talk about it, as it wasn't every day that someone built a new house there. Shonnie Mòr called it the 'Rona Castle' and, in one verse, he mentioned that the biblical tower of Babel was nothing compared to the Rona Castle. His love songs to my grandmother were especially beautiful, especially one he composed after her death at an early age. These were songs from deep within his heart telling of his love, joy and sorrow. Another couple of songs were composed about the Boer War and the First World War.

One especially amusing song, but not amusing to him, was one composed deploring the fact that a law had been passed banning the tarring of sheep, which had always been the custom to prevent maggot fly. Now all sheep had to be dipped, and Shonnie Mòr was quite sure that that would be detrimental to the quality of the Highland Tweed.

Who's to say that he may not have been right? Whatever, Shonnie Mòr ended up in court at Portree on Skye and, in one verse of the song, he bemoans the fact that the Fiscal, 'that shameless one', was miscalling him to the Sheriff. When I hear what passes for songs today,

I wonder what Shonnie Mòr would have said of them. This grand old man looked like one of the Patriarchs from the Old Testament, at least according to the pictures in my father's family bible. Shonnie Mòr had a weather-beaten, kindly face with a white-ish grey beard, but there the patriarchal resemblance ended. He usually wore what would be called serge or moleskin trousers and a naval type jumper. Of course, when I knew him, he had mellowed quite a bit. My mother used to relate some of his escapades of the time when she was young.

One such story was about the time when the family were young and money really was very scarce. My grandmother looked forward to the time when the spare cow would be sold. At sale time, big Shonnie took the cow to Portree sales, presumably in a rowing boat, and returned home with very little to show from the sale of the cow. My mother told me, "Granny was ready to give him a row" as he stepped ashore from the boat. I imagine she was eagerly waiting for the money. Shonnie Mòr forestalled her by jumping ashore and giving her a warm embrace with the words, "Kirsty, I love you."

What could a woman do after such a greeting?

EILEAN TIGHE

As we now had crossed over to Eilean Tighe and walked the well known path to the house, which was just a ruin, and as I gazed at its old walls, in spite of the dilapidation and the bracken growing inside, scenes of my childhood became quite vivid. I looked where the fireplace used to be, the chimney head and face stone were still in place, and I could see Shonnie Mòr sitting at the corner of the fireplace on his homemade four-legged stool, always humming to himself. It was only in later years that I realised that he must have been composing his Gaelic songs. I can remember how, if we were in any kind of trouble and expecting a telling off, we always found refuge behind 'Seanair's' (grandfather in Gaelic) stool.

The house was thatched with heather thatch. I can picture it very clearly, with very thick heather-twisted ropes fixed from one side to the other, and at each side where the thatch ended, slightly overlapping the walls, was tied a heavy stone. This was to keep the thatch intact in winter storms. The house was also unusual in that it was the only house that I knew on the Island of Raasay, or indeed anywhere around, that had rounded corners, I understand that was to lessen the effect of the strong winter storms on this exposed island. It had very small windows and just three rooms. There was the kitchen-cum-dining room-cum-bedroom at one end, and in the middle, a small bedroom called the closet. At the other end, was quite a large bedroom. Grandfather slept in the closet, mother and father in the hole-in-the-wall bed in the kitchen, and all the children slept in the end room. I can remember at times sleeping at the foot of the bed with one of my sisters, while two more slept at the head, literally like sardines. The living-cum-bedroom-cum-dining quarters had what is known as a hanging chimney place, with the chimneybreast jutting out from the wall; the fire of peat was laid on a flat stone inside this. A very convenient arrangement, as one could sit at the sides as well as the front. The peat gave off a lovely aroma as it burned, to think of it makes for nostalgia. Hanging inside the huge chimney was a strong chain called a 'Slabhraidh' in the Gaelic; this was attached to a strong iron crossbar further up the chimney. At the end of the 'Slabhraidh', was a strong hook on which the kettle would hang to boil and the bow handled skillets, griddle and strong large frying pan. All these cooking utensils had these bow handles for hanging on the hook. The handles were called 'bùlasg' and the rate of boiling was controlled by putting the pot on a higher link of the chain by raising the hook. It was all very effective, but by burning so much peat, the chimney got very sooty, so the cook had to be very careful that everything had a lid on. If you lifted the lid to check the food, sure, at that time an avalanche of soot would come down, and believe me sooty potatoes in their jackets is a taste you never forget – it is just vile. However, in those hard days we couldn't afford to throw them out. One of my aunts swore by this soot for cleaning teeth, and I have seen her take it from the chimney for this purpose; she had beautiful teeth well into old age. She was probably the only one who cleaned her teeth, as she had been away to Glasgow in 'service' and would have got used to modern habits. I can never remember owning a toothbrush at that stage. We did have some when we lived in Kyle Rona, provided by a cousin from Glasgow who came home on holiday.

To describe more about the house itself. There was no ceiling as such, only a few planks placed across the joists, which served as a useful store for our fishing nets and tackle. The fun began when we had a heavy rain and maybe some of the thatch needed repairing, but whatever the cause, we had a bad time with the 'Black Rain' (Sileadh dubh), because of the high soot content as the rain came through the thatch, it collected years of accumulation of peat smoke (it didn't always go up the chimney). Various bowls and buckets would be placed on the floor to catch the drips, though I could never see why, as there was no real floor, just a few flagstones here and there, worn smooth by years of human feet. It doesn't sound very hygienic, but strange to say, we suffered very few illnesses.

Underneath the curtained hole-in-the-wall-bed, were kept the winter's stock of potatoes and also the seed potatoes for the following spring. It was a very safe place from the frost, but often mice had some good dinners off them too. Thinking of seed potatoes reminds me that father never, to my knowledge, bought seed potatoes; he would sit at planting time and cut the eyes out with a good piece of potato attached and this is what he planted. My, what a lovely crop of potatoes he got. He was also very exact about the planting of them. When we helped him, after he had turned over a furrow of soil with the 'cas chròm' (foot plough), he would give us a piece of stick and that was to be the distance to set each potato from the other. Betty and I used to drop in two together when he wasn't looking, intending to look them up later on to see what would happen. Of course, by the time the crop was ripe, we had forgotten. My brother John often had to stay at home for weeks from school to help with the spring work and harvest. Seemingly, it was allowed in those days. When the harvest was safely gathered in and the dark winter nights arrived, there was no radio or television to pass the time, but there were always Gaelic stories to relate, usually ghostly ones.

Father had some very hair-raising ones, too, of actual ghostly happenings, some of his young days and in later life. You see, he was one of these unusual people with the 'Second Sight'. I believe it was a gift he would rather not have had.

The wintertime was also the time for corn grinding. This was done with a pair of corn millstones called a Quern or a 'Bràdh'. It consisted of two round stones, with a hole in the centre of the top one. The corn, usually oats, was first hardened by placing near the fire, and then put into the hole in the middle. There was also a hollow in the edge of the top stone, into which a long pole was placed, which was then turned by hand. The two stones had previously been placed on a clean piece of sacking or tarpaulin if available, and the ground meal was forced out the sides and collected from the tarpaulin. This meal was darker than ordinary, bought oatmeal and it had a wonderful nutty taste, ideal for oatcakes. Of course, in my young days, mother made all her own scones and oatcakes – bread was unknown to us till much later. Butter was also made by hand, in a large churn with a handle at the front that turned a double ladder type of paddle inside and we all took turns to work the handle. Sometimes, if the cream was not so plentiful, the butter was made in a crock jar with a wooden thumper, which was pumped up and down to agitate the cream. I recall one time a very sad occasion. It happened like this – mother collected the cream as usual from the top of the milk, which often had been standing for a few days. If there was enough for the big churn, it all got tipped into that. But this day, I think mother must have been in a hurry and wasn't as careful as she usually was, because she failed to see that a dead mouse was in the cream. Obviously, it had drowned while investigating the lovely meal. Mother did not discover the mouse (in bits) until the cream had been well beaten and the lot had to be thrown out. What made matters worse, was the fact that mother was terrified of mice, dead or alive.

Another winter night's work was mending the nets ready for the fishing. Father would suspend the net from a beam and with his ball of twine and mending hook, he was an expert at it. During the war years, he made hair-nets for my mother from knitting wool. These 'snoods', as they were called, were very popular at the time. Thinking of these winter nights brings to mind a lovely homely scene – father mending his nets and mother in the corner with her spinning wheel, making her own knitting wool, ready for making socks and jumpers for the family and, during the War years, many woollen comforts for the servicemen. One memory I'd rather forget was the crickets. These horrible creatures like mini-locusts, lived in the walls of the house and especially in crevices in the fireplace. When the oil lamp was lit at night, they began chirping, I didn't mind that so much as when they decided to take a flying leap across the room, sometimes landing on your shoulder or your head. I shiver even at the thought of them. I often wondered what became of them when the house was left empty. I don't think they would survive without the warmth, but I don't feel any pity for them.

As I sat on a hill near our old home, I thought of our parents and the hard life they lived, with no home comforts whatsoever, and yet so contented with their lot. I believe their contentment had a lot to do with their strong faith in God. I can still hear father reading morning and evening from the Bible, and us all joining in the singing of a Psalm, all in Gaelic. He always ended with a fervent Prayer of Thanksgiving for the life and health and all provision for his family, also praying that we would know Christ as our Saviour.

I think I may be unique in that I can remember my own Christening, or Baptism, as it was known in our Church. I don't know how old I was, but several of us were baptised at the same time. We had to go by boat to the Church in Torran. I have a recollection of being carried upon a gentleman's shoulder up from the shore to the Church. I believe the gentleman was my Uncle James who was living with us at the time; he was my father's brother.

My poor mother must have had a really busy life, bringing up a big family and catering for these men folk. The washing alone must have been daunting, no automatic washing machine or tumble dryer, just *Sunlight Soap*, washboard, and hot water in a big wooden tub. But her work didn't finish there; she also helped on the land, carrying manure and seaweed for fertilizer in a creel on her back. The creels were also used for carrying the peat home. How often I watched her bringing home the peat, knitting at the same time and usually very complicated 'Fair Isle' patterns. She used to make lovely long stockings that men wore with the then popular 'plus fours'.

I would now like to tell you about these useful 'Creels'. They were all homemade in my young days, usually by Grandfather. They were a real work of art, and it was fascinating to watch. The main canes were stuck into the ground and then the rest were woven in and out until the creel was the right size.

Now, we are outside once more and I can help you to see why this Island has such a special place in my heart. We are standing at the front of the house and looking across to the Island of Rona and various other small islands, it is an unforgettable view. On occasions, the sea is wild and restless, with white-capped, huge waves that toss and turn and dash against the rocks on the shore. At other times, it is serene and peaceful, with the reflections of the little isles and hills in the water. Around are heather-covered hills, and beyond the stretch of sea, the mainland of Scotland. Looking down past Rona is the wild sea called the 'Minch'; this looks to the Outer Hebrides. I'm sure there cannot be many places left today with such wild but serene beauty. To me, these lovely hills and Islands call out for human companionship – it was never meant to be unseen and not enjoyed by man. I wonder if this lovely spot will ever again know the joy of children's voices and human habitation.

When I mentioned the wild 'Minch' just now, I was reminded once again of my father. He was a fearless seaman, although he couldn't swim, but the sea seemed to hold no terrors for him. He was a postman to the lighthouse on the Isle of Rona for many years. The delivery of the lighthouse mail was accomplished only, many times, after a stormy, hazardous journey. While living in Kyle Rona after I left school, I sometimes made the crossing with him, helping to row the boat to Rona and carry excess mail on my back. The lighthouse people got a lot of parcels from friends and packages of magazines and newspapers. After getting to Rona, we had several miles to walk – about six miles – but, when we got to the lighthouse, we got a great welcome from the keeper and assistant. In my time, the assistant keeper was a Mr. Crowe who was looked after by his sister. She was a very good baker, and we always had really sumptuous cakes with a cup of tea. In later years, the lighthouse was our only real communication with the outside world.

At the beginning of the 1939 War, when we had not yet got a radio, not many people had, the lighthouse had its own radio communications. So the latest war news was written down for my father, and when we got home, I in turn would write the 'News' down for John MacLeod, the man who brought the mails from Arnish to Kyle Rona, and that is how the war news was circulated to the Arnish and Torran folk.

On one occasion, father came very near to drowning. It was a very stormy day, and the harder he rowed the more tired he got. The storm became a roaring gale and he soon was drifting down towards the wild 'Minch'. There was nothing he could do but let the boat drift, as it was too stormy to do anything else. Eventually, a fishing boat came to the rescue and took his wee boat in tow. I was with him myself on another wild day, although it started off quite calm, but I think father must have expected it to get a bit stormy for, instead of going to his usual landing place, which was Big Harbour, he took it to 'Port an Teampall' – in English, the Temple Port, which was a much shorter crossing. We got across without any bother and delivered the mail, both to the MacRaes at Big Harbour and to the lighthouse. At the MacRae's, he always got a cup of tea to set him on his journey to the lighthouse, but I wasn't very keen on Flora MacRae's tea. She lived here with her two old brothers for as long as I could remember. I believe they originally came from Kyleakin. Flora looked as if she could do with a good scrub, so I never fancied drinking out of the grimy cups. The brothers James and Christopher were a quaint couple. James seemed very scholarly and quite smart, compared with Christopher, who didn't seem to care how he dressed. It was quite usual to see him going about with a safety pin holding his trouser fly closed.

After coming back from the lighthouse, we could see the wind was getting up and, by the time we reached 'Port an Teampall', it was a real storm. We waited for a while to see if it would calm down, but as it looked like getting worse, father decided it was best to row across to

Eilean Tighe as it was the nearest shore, (at this time we were living in Kyle Rona). It was from there we rowed across in the morning, but getting to Eilean Tighe was not so easy. I think he could see I was a bit scared, as the boat got caught in between huge waves and we didn't seem to be making any progress. I was using one oar and he the other. He just kept telling me to put all my strength into the rowing; I think he thought that the effort would make me forget the roaring sea around me. Maybe it did to a certain extent, but I was still frightened. I couldn't swim either and, even if I could, we were miles from shore, in the middle of winter, in a wild stormy gale. However, eventually we were drawing closer to land, but the swell had carried us far beyond where he intended to get. We eventually got the boat near enough, and oh, what a relief, there on the shore was my cousin Angus from Glasgow, who was staying with us. He was a very strong swimmer and, as we couldn't get too near the shore, he swam out to us and took over from me at the oars. I couldn't have gone any further I don't think. Angus had come to look for us and, finding the tide in at the Caolas (Kyle) of Eilean Tighe, he swam across and walked to this point, where he saw us. My poor mother and my aunt (Angus' mother) met us on our way home, both of them in tears; they thought we were lost. That was an ordeal I never forgot.

We now wander down to a little hillock by the seashore in front of the old house at Eilean Tighe. This was where my sisters and I so many years ago watched the seagulls, soaring and screeching overhead, or a beautiful dive by a solan – goose – to retrieve his dinner from beneath the waves. Sometimes, a seal would appear to swim lazily around, turning his head from side to side, as if listening to our conversation. At times, I have walked over to the 'Caolas' and watched an otter in its own inimitable style come sliding down, to twist and turn and just to play for the sheer fun of it. How we always enjoyed going along the shore, turning stones and finding small crabs and fish. We also collected dulse, which is an edible seaweed.

There is a strange sequel to this beachcombing. It happened before I was old enough to do this kind of pastime myself, so I relate it as my mother told me later on. Apparently, my oldest sister, Peggy, and the next one, Chrissie, went beachcombing and came running home to mother to tell her with worried faces, "We have found a Red Indian Baby on the shore." Mother hurried along to look at this body and found not a baby, but a two pronged carrot! They saw what they took to be a baby's legs sticking out of the seaweed, got a fright and didn't wait to look for the head of the baby. They wouldn't know what a carrot was, as the only vegetables grown on the island were potatoes, turnips and sometimes cabbage. How they knew what colour a Red Indian baby was, I don't know. I loved beachcombing. I remember once finding a strange round bulb, which I brought home and planted, and it grew very tall with a beautiful seed and flower. I now know it was an onion. There were such wonders we had never seen – an electric light bulb, which we just could not imagine what it was for, and then there were lots of round glass floats, which came in handy for father's nets. We lived a very simple, but extremely happy life.

It was on Eilean Tighe that I saw my very first aeroplane; at least I think it was a bi-plane. We were working at the peats, father cutting and we children helping, when we heard this eerie drone. We were a bit scared, as at first, we couldn't see anything, and then father shouted, "soitheach adhair" (airship). This was something we hadn't heard of before, let alone seen. Father must have heard the name airship somewhere, probably from one of the newspapers friends sent home from Glasgow. My favourite paper was the '*Bulletin*' because it had such a lot of pictures in it. The stories in it wouldn't mean much to me then, as I couldn't read anyway, and I could only speak Gaelic except for a few English words learned from my Glasgow cousins.

We didn't know much about Christmas at all. I can't remember celebrating it in any way, but at New Year, relations from Glasgow sent parcels. A special treat was when my father's brother, Uncle John who worked in a large grocery shop in Glasgow (I believe later he was manager there), used to send us a tea-chest full of all kinds of goodies, which normally we couldn't afford and couldn't get on the island. There were iced cakes, tea, sweets, oranges etc., but our great delight was the tinfoil that the chest was lined with. From this foil, we fashioned cups and saucers to play 'house' with.

We took great pleasure in making our own amusements. I remember another cousin who was a great favourite with us was Angus' sister, Margaret. Now Margaret Talloch, she loved taking us all out for picnics. We never knew what she would produce for 'eats', as she brought lovely things home with her – things again that were a luxury to us, such as shortbread, chocolate bars and, for sandwiches, jars of meat paste. We always ended up somewhere by the shore, and we really appreciated everything so much, because we had so little. Yet, we had the most precious thing of all, happiness and a lovely Christian home. Margaret once brought me home a swimsuit, made of fine blue rubber, I was so proud of it, no-one had anything like that. We used to go and dip in the sea at the Caolas where it was shallow, but we couldn't swim.

Two dim memories I have are of a 'bull' being towed behind a boat coming from Rona, which was the usual way. The bull was, I believe, on loan from the department of agriculture, and was sent to different townships on the island. I remember watching a bull brought across; the poor animal's head could just be seen above the water. I think someone must have been holding his head up. I wonder what would have happened if he had tried to clamber into the boat.

I also have a dim memory of one of the last families to leave the Island of Rona; they were Donald Nicolson's family. The Nicolson family left in a rowing boat and we watched them going through the Caolas at Eilean Tighe. The boat was piled high with possessions; the larger furniture must have been sent on earlier on a larger boat. We waved to them as they went through the Caolas. I expect they felt quite sad. The only people left on Rona now were the MacRae brothers and their sister Flora, and they didn't leave until about 1942.

The reader will wonder how young children passed the time without T.V., radio and very few toys of any kind. We had vivid imaginations and, as I've already said, used our imaginations to amuse ourselves. One pastime, which we loved, was what we called 'tighean beaga' – 'little houses' in Gaelic. We collected broken bits of crockery, especially pretty ones, also old kettles, pots and pans, and each chose a suitable spot with ledges or crevices to display our wares. Then, we just became ordinary housewives and visited each other, entertaining our visitors with 'pretend' tea, etc. I believe this was very good, as it taught us to improvise, something I find useful now. One year, mother told us that a maiden aunt, who was very severe in her outlook and hadn't much sympathy with wee girls playing houses, (we remembered that at one time she had thrown away our precious crockery, etc.) was paying us a visit. Well, we were not about to let Mairie Mhòr do that again, so before she came home, we carted all our worldly goods and did a flitting to a cave some distance away.

A very exciting pastime, when there was a very low tide, was 'mùsgain gathering' (mùsgain is Gaelic for razor fish). Mother was really adept at it; her instructions to us were as follows. "Realise first of all that razor fish disappear back into the sand at the least sound of footsteps or any movement. Next, never use anything metal to dig them out with – when you locate one, dig it out with a suitable piece of wood".

She also used to whistle to them when she was getting them out. You had to work fast, as they quickly slid back into the sand. They actually seemed to respond to whistling. Now, come to think of it, it wasn't exactly whistling, but more a pursing of the lips with a sucking in noise like sometimes we use for calling a dog. These razor fish make delicious eating, tasting very like scallops. Of course, we had to live mostly from the sea and our own produce. Father had a shotgun and used it to good effect to shoot cormorants and wild duck. The cormorant made good scotch broth, but the meat was a bit 'fishy'. But, if it was skinned instead of plucked, it was quite palatable.

Sometimes, both at Eilean Tighe and Kyle Rona, father took us to one of the little rocky islands between Eilean Tighe and Rona; I think mostly when he was doing the trip to Rona Lighthouse anyway. This was in order to collect sea bird eggs. There would be dozens of nests just on little grassy patches between the rocks. The birds were mostly different types of seagulls, ducks, sandpipers, oyster-catchers and terns. When we brought them home, we put them in a bowl of water. The drill was, if they floated they were discarded – I suppose these would have a chick in them. If they sank, they were good for eating, and my, they really were the best eggs I've ever tasted.

Our main food was fish and potatoes, but I have known when the weather was bad and father couldn't get any fish, our winter stock of salted and dried fish was exhausted. We then had to fall back on just potatoes and milk, two items always available. But even this frugal meal became an adventure. Mother boiled a huge pot of potatoes, mashed them up with plenty of butter till beautiful and creamy, and then piled them in a mound on a large meat plate. Each child sat round the table with a small bowl of milk and dug our way into the potato mountain with a spoon. What excitement, as we tunnelled through to meet each other inside. I'm sure the fun of it made us forget the meagreness of the meal.

Eilean Tighe was a very beautiful little island, but not very fertile. I can picture now the tiny cuts of land my father used to till with the 'Cas Chròm' (foot plough). It must have been backbreaking work. I recall one strip of ground, which we called the 'faoileann' the exact meaning of which I am not sure, but certainly something to do with the sea. I know that a seagull is sometimes called by this name in Gaelic. I believe this strip of land was the most fertile, perhaps because in it, the soil was copiously mixed with shingle. Maybe this part was at one time covered by the sea, hence the sea-type name. A lot of the island was covered in beautiful heather and gorse. Well, if you don't know anything about gorse, I can tell you it has very vicious thorns, and when it is dying down in the autumn, they drop off onto the ground.

I know because we had to be careful going about in our bare feet – shoes were for the bad weather, or should I say boots, as these were a luxury kept for the winter.

My mother often told me a very amusing story about gorse thorns. It happened in my grandmother's time, I believe. Seemingly, Cousin Donald was home from Glasgow, I expect for the school holidays. Donald and my oldest brother, James, were playing outside; they must have been near gorse bushes, probably where they were not meant to go. Donald fell down on his bottom and got some gorse thorns embedded in that part of his anatomy. So, the bright lads sneaked indoors into the end room, which also acted as a bedroom.

In the centre of the room was a large table with grandmother's beautiful treasured oil lamp. I have a good knowledge of this lamp myself as mother had it for many years. It had a lovely pink glass bowl for the oil, with a raised floral pattern and, covering the wick, was a glass funnel. Over that, a magnificent, figured-glass, round lamp globe, something that would be very much sought after at the auctions today. Donald clambered onto the table in an appropriate posture, in order that James, with either a pin or a needle, probably a safety pin, could remove the gorse thorns. But, oh dear, at the first stab of the pin, Donald jumped, and hit the globe off the lamp. Of course, it wasn't made for such rough treatment and it landed on the floor in smithereens. I never heard what punishment the boys received. But I would imagine that, after relieving Donald of the offending thorns, they both would have more than the pain of the thorns to think about.

Some very hilarious things happened in that old house at Eilean Tighe. I recall at one time, mother must have been given a pair of slippers with a fur trim. Now, in our living room, there was a wooden settle with arms at the ends. Most houses on the island had them, as we had never heard of armchairs and settees. Underneath the settle was a space for shoes and slippers. It was dark under the settle and the old oil lamp had not yet been lit, so I put my hand under and felt around for the slippers. When I located them, or one of them, I pulled it out and to my horror, found I had pulled out an old shoe with a dead rat inside. I can still feel the revulsion I felt. Seemingly, father had put down some rat poison, as the rats sometimes came in to pinch the potatoes, and the horrible rodent had come in to die in the shoe.

I think that same bench has painful memories for my sister Betty. We were playing about one evening on the settle, when all of a sudden she toppled over the wooden arm into a pail of very near boiling calves' supper (oilcake and boiling water) mother had got ready to take out to one of the calves and had stood it there to cool. You can imagine Betty's cries as she not only got a terrible fright, but also was scalded.

Sometimes, on Sunday evenings, we would pass the time by looking at the pictures in father's large Gaelic '*Pilgrims Progress*'. One picture must have especially taken brother John's fancy. It was Satan, or Appolyon as he was named in the caption; he was shown hovering above Christian as he was kneeling praying. Mother told us sometime after, how she came upon John and Chrissie enacting the story. She heard John say to Chrissie, "You be Christian and I'll be Satan hovering above you!"

An experience I painfully remember was when Betty and I went down to 'Cnoc an Fhalasgair' the 'Bonfire Hillock'. Apparently, this was where a bonfire was lit as a signal that someone wanted to be ferried to Rona or vice versa. There was a similar place on the other side. I had never seen the one on Eilean Tighe side used, but I can remember father going across to Rona when he saw a signal fire on the other side. Anyway, Betty and I decided to sit down here near the shore, as it was a beautiful day, but we didn't sit for long. We had sat on a red anthill and our bottoms were severely stung. Then, we saw a huge rubber tyre that had been washed ashore and had been lying in the scorching sun for some time. Oh, what a relief to sit our bare bottoms on the hot rubber. It certainly eased the agony.

My sister, Chrissie, always seemed to be in the wars. On one occasion, she was down at the shore with John and Peggy to collect driftwood for the fire, and Chrissie found an old plank, maybe a bit of a boat, and sat on it. She never said anything, but when she got home later, Chrissie, as we often did, sat on the hearthstone in front of the fire. She hadn't realised that the piece of wood on which she had sat at the shore, was tarry, and when mother called her, presumably for supper, she was stuck fast (knickers were unheard of on Eilean Tighe in those days). Mother could not understand why she didn't move and she was too scared to say. At last, mother investigated and Chrissie ended up being de-tarred with paraffin.

Chrissie was also very inquisitive. Once when mother had been away to the south end of Raasay, where there was a shop, she brought back a couple of dolls for Chrissie and me. I can see them now. They were a kind of rag doll, but made of oilcloth, and unfortunately for my doll, they had a squeak when pressed. One day, I went to get my doll to play with, but Chrissie had operated on her to find where the squeak came from. She had cut a hole in the back and pulled out the wood shavings, with which it was filled. Fortunately, mother was able to do a repair job on it, but it never seemed to be the same after that.

Another time she washed her hands, and came to mother looking for something to dry them on. There was usually some kind of towel hanging on a nail behind the door, so mother told her in Gaelic, to use a portion of the towel. Before she could be stopped, she had with her sharp teeth torn a piece out of the towel – she took it all literally.

I recall an amusing incident that happened when my sister Malina, the youngest, was born. As was usual, because of the remoteness of our home, the midwife came and stayed for a week or so before the baby arrived. This midwife was the only one ever on the Island, and was at least a trained one. She originally lived on the Island of Rona and the Island owner's wife, who was then a Mrs. Woods, saw some potential in this lady, so she paid for her to go away to be trained as a midwife. Her name was Bella MacLeod and was then a widow. Her son was the very well known John MacLeod, 'the Shoemaker of Clachan Raasay'; his family and grandchildren still live on Raasay. This Bella MacLeod must have been a wonderful nurse to have been able to carry out her work under conditions that prevailed at that time. She first had to come by pony and trap to Brochel Castle, and then walk eight or nine miles to Eilean Tighe. I can't remember if, this time, she might have come by boat, but that was certainly not always the case. There was no electricity or hot water, except by boiling kettles on the peat fire, and most importantly, no doctor within calling distance in case of an emergency. Bella duly arrived at our house and I think I must have been misbehaving, or said something she didn't approve of, because she told me if I didn't behave, I wouldn't see what she had in her bag. Of course, we children all knew that there was a baby in the bag; that was how they arrived!

* * *

Sometimes my sister, Betty, and I went for long rambles over the hills and moors. I recall one windy day (it had to be for this game) climbing up to the top of Meall Mòr and setting off the most extraordinary craft you ever saw. It was called a 'Gòlan Gaoithe', which is actually the Gaelic for a swallow. The Gòlan Gaoithe was made from a large raw potato, with either hen's or seagull's feathers stuck into it all over. You needed a good strong wind to fly these strange craft, but when the wind caught them and they flew away, it was very exciting, but you never got them back. I often wondered if they had landed on a passing steamer, what they might have made of them – maybe extinct birds, or things from outer space. Of course, we had to make our own amusement, as toys were unknown things, but we were so happy with very little.

I mentioned earlier about the 'tarring of sheep', which was done to prevent ticks, lice and maggot fly. Sheep tarring night was a great occasion. During the day, the menfolk, joined by men from the neighbouring Isle of Fladda, also from Arnish and Torran, would roam the Island to bring the sheep in to the pen. Some would be housed in the peat shed at the end of the house; the living room was the tarring room.

Just picture the scene. The room would have been cleared of the usual furniture to make room for the 'smearing stools' – 'smearing' was what the tarring was called. The tarring stool was a long wooden slatted contraption tapered at one end, long enough to lay a sheep on it. The man sat astride at the broader end with the sheep laid out in front and a bucket of tar on the floor beside them. He would part the coat or fleece in sections and smear dollops of tar on by hand. This was done all over the fleece. You can imagine the smell of sheep and tar that pervaded the house then, and for days afterwards, but somehow we didn't seem to notice it; it was part of living. Maybe the reader can now appreciate why there was no floor covering.

TO PASS THE TIME ON A WINTER'S EVENING

As there was no T.V. or Radio to pass the time, especially on winter nights, the usual pastime for the older folk when someone came to call, or 'Ceilidh' as it is called in Gaelic, was the telling of stories of things that happened in their own young days. Of course, we listened in on these stories, and one I specially remember father telling was of the time he and his brother, my Uncle Donald, were sitting up at night with an old lady who was dying. While they sat there, suddenly a cat came walking in and sat over beside the old lady's bed. What a cat, with beautiful long silky fur, the like had never been seen on the Island. But that was not all. It was followed by (I'm not sure if my memory is correct on the number) five more of the same kind and they all took their place by the bedside. Uncle Donald took up a lump of peat which lay on the hearth to throw at them, when the dying old woman shouted, "Don't touch them, they are my friends."

In later years, I asked him about the episode and he assured me it happened just as he told it, but he could not give any explanation for it. I should add that actually the old lady was understood by many at that time to be a witch.

Another story father used to tell was of one moonlit night when he and his brothers were young in Doire Dubh. They were out in front of the house, playing football, when a ball of fire appeared from nowhere and weaved its way between them and then disappeared. The lads got a fright and went indoors. When father went to look next day, the grass was burnt where the fireball had rolled. Could this have been some kind of meteorite, I wonder? Of course, father had the gift of 'Second Sight'. Many people speak of this as just a fantasy, or a kind of 'old wives tale', but I can vouch for the truth of it. It was a gift he did not desire and something he never spoke about himself. My mother told that, on many occasions, he knew beforehand that something was going to happen, usually connected with accidents or death.

The one time this happened in my own lifetime was when my mother's brother, Uncle John Nicolson was killed when he fell off a lorry when it was going round a bad bend on the road to the Pier at the south end of Raasay. Uncle John had retired after a lifetime in the police force in Glasgow. I was away from home, in the Services, when the accident happened, but I was told about it by mother when I came home on leave. She told me that, sometime before the accident, she was walking home from church with father one dark night, when he suddenly caught her by the arm and pulled her to the side of this narrow road, saying that a motor was coming towards them. Seemingly, he saw its lights. Mother did not see or hear anything and no vehicle passed them, and father was silent about it afterwards – until the day of the accident when he was sent for from their home nearby, to help. He knew straightaway that was what he saw that dark night. A very strange story indeed, but one I know to be true, for father was a good Christian man, who would never make up such a story.

One more story, which I heard him tell, was that, on his way home from fishing one dark night, as he was passing Norman Mackenzies house (mentioned earlier), he heard pigs grunting and he was quite adamant that it was nothing else but pigs. Now, that might not seem strange today, but I don't believe there was a pig on the island, let alone in Kyle Rona. So far as I know, nothing has come of this strange happening, but as I thought about it recently, it doesn't seem impossible or incredible. Norman Mackenzie's old house has been re-roofed and refurbished inside to become a backpackers 'bothy'. Maybe, just maybe, one of the backpackers had a portable radio. Could this not have been a farming programme on, which could be heard outside? But in this day and age, nothing is impossible. After all, no-one would even dream that that old ruin, which was derelict for about fifty years, would now be a lovely renovated 'bothy'. Could be that, in the future, these lonely derelict townships could be inhabited again, and why not a farm nearby? It's just a thought.

I was now brought back to the present with a call from Arthur and John that we must hurry back to the Caolas, as the tide was coming in, but I felt very reluctant to leave my lovely island with its many memories. As I took a last look at the old ruins, I noticed the cave above the house. It was called 'Johnson's Cave'. I have often wondered why, as Johnson was not a name known either in Rona, Eilean Tighe or Raasay. But, whatever the reason for the name, it was a great place for playing games in my young days. Looking at it now, I couldn't help thinking how dangerous it was. It was set high in the rock face, the entrance reached by a narrow ledge. We used to chase each other back and forth across the ledge, yet a slip and we would have been over the edge and onto the rocks below.

So, we leave this memory-filled island of my dreams and the sad ruins of my birthplace. If these rocks could talk, what stories they would tell of the folk who lived here, long since gone, the hardship they endured, but their happiness with their lot, (no keeping up with the

Jones there), but just love of home and family and a deep contentment and faith in God. Life was hard, the pleasures of life were simple, but sometimes I yearn for the peace of those days in the rat race and clockwatching of modern living.

We crossed the Caolas before the tide came back in and started our long walk back. Now and then on the return journey, I kept looking back just once more to see the well-loved outline of Eilean Tighe.

THE WALK BACK FROM EILEAN TIGHE

Winding our way back to Arnish, we again passed the old house in Kyle Rona and, looking up at the hill above the house, I had another glimpse, in my mind of how things were in those days. For instance, if we needed meal, which we got in 1cwt bags, or flour for mother's never-ending scone making, it usually was sent away for to a firm in Greenock – I think the name was *Macfarlanes*. Then, a ship called the '*Sweet Home*' brought it to us, along with provisions for other Islands. As there wasn't a jetty in Kyle Rona, the ship just blew its siren and father got the wee boat out, went alongside and took our goods on board. We had been notified of the ships due date of call. One time, father played a naughty trick on my brother, James, and a pal who was staying with us. Father had a cow horn that he had fashioned into a kind of trumpet; it gave a very good imitation of a ships siren. This day, James and Kenny MacKenzie, his pal, said when the '*Sweet Home*' arrived they would take the wee boat out to meet it. So, father blew his cow horn hard, and the unsuspecting lads ran for the shore, quite a distance away to meet the 'Sweet Home'. I don't remember now, how far they got before they realised they had been fooled.

When we got to Arnish, we called at Calum MacLeod, the roadmaker. Calum's wife had been the schoolteacher at Torran, but after we had all left school. This very generous couple set before us a well-laden table of potatoes, stewed rabbit and vegetables, and to follow, tea, scones, jam and oatcake with fresh homemade butter. What a welcome treat that was, as by this time, we were all getting very hungry. Here we spent a couple of hours, just talking to Calum about the 'old days'. He was a mine of information on most subjects. He won a gold medal for writing about a relation of his who lived many years before. This essay was all in Gaelic; he also was awarded the M.B.E. for his roadmaking.

At the time of meeting him, he was writing a book, in Gaelic, about different men of Raasay. I may not have the title correct, but I think he was going to call it '*Great Men of Raasay*'. I believe Calum died before it was published, and I don't know if his family saw to its publication afterwards. I hope they did.

Walking back to Brochel Castle on that beautiful summer evening was something never to be forgotten. Looking across to the Cullin Hills of Skye was like looking at a beautifully worked tapestry. The hills were all shades of blues and purple, the calm blue sea between Skye and us. I couldn't help thinking how different it could be; it could very quickly turn to the wild and cruel sea, such as my father encountered on his trips to Rona on those winter days long ago. But a wild sea with white crested waves, seemingly furious at the rocks it swept up against, had to my mind its own beauty, and I still think that to hear the sound of the waves dashing against the shore is something I will always associate with my childhood.

Peter was waiting for us as promised at Brochel Castle and, by now, we were glad to rest our feet and get conveyed by car back home to Inverarish. I might never visit Kyle Rona or Eilean Tighe again, but my wish is that by writing about my happy childhood, this long forgotten way of life will come to life again as people read this book. Maybe in this busy world of mixed up values today, no-one will understand how anyone could be happy living in such primitive circumstances, but that's because they have never felt the magic of living where time has no meaning, and all things that matter are free.

Kyle Rona House

"The Lonely Mariner", my father in his wee boat

My father on a visit to Glasgow

Peat cutting on Eilean Tighe, brother John, grandfather Seonaidh Mòr and father

Seonaidh Mòr's wife, Granny Nicolson

Mother and Uncle John, so tragically killed on Raasay

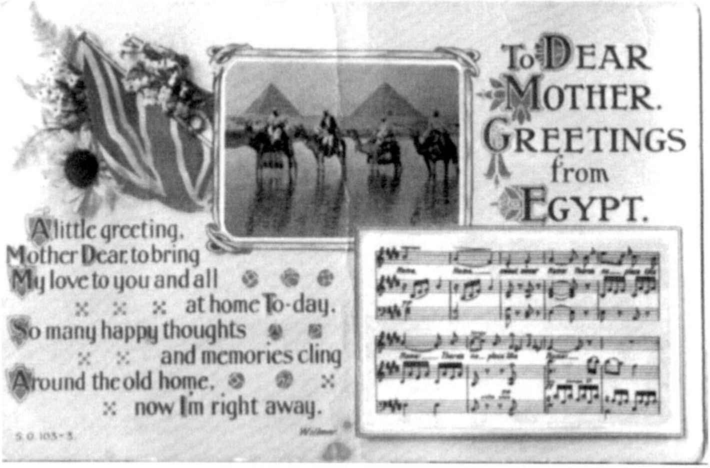

Postcard from Uncle John to his mother, Granny Nicolson at the end of World War 1

Father and friend in the Kyle at Eilean Tighe

Ruins of ancestral home on Eilean Tighe

Ruins of Brochel Castle

Brother John at Kyle Rona, pre-War

Mother with the District Nurse at Kyle Rona House

The Rona Lighthouse

My mother spinning outside Kyle Rona House

Seonaidh Mòr, my grandfather, the Gaelic Bard

Seonaidh Mòr with handmade rake

Picnic on Eilean Tighe

with Cousin Margaret, her niece and nephews. The niece second from the right was later killed in the bombing of Glasgow; Margaret is on the left with her arm round me, sister Betty on the right

The school house in Torran

My paternal grandmother, Peggy Cumming

The church in Torran

My brother John with the cas chróm (foot plough)

The family at Eilean Tighe

L to R: John, Chrissie, Betty, myself and Peggy holding Malina

WAR EFFORT

In 1941, I thought I really ought to be doing something for the war effort, so, although I was actually exempt from military service, because my father was a crofter, I joined the A.T.S. (Auxiliary Territorial Service) as a volunteer.

In my case, it was an easy matter to join up; I simply completed and signed an enlistment form from the Scottish newspaper, the '*People's Journal*'. What a different world was opened up to me. This was really an eye-opener in many ways, for up till then, my knowledge of the outside world, as you can imagine, was very limited.

When my 'calling up' papers came through, I was instructed to report to Newbattle Abbey, Dalkeith, near Edinburgh. Up till that time, I had been only once on a train and that only a short trip. This journey meant going by ship to the mainland, which was no bother; I had done that many times. The daunting part was that I then had to go by train to Glasgow and on to Edinburgh.

My Aunt Mary, mentioned earlier, met me at Buchanan Street station in Glasgow and I was so relieved to see a face I knew. Everywhere seemed so terribly noisy, including the people. Aunt Mary was different; she still had an island twang. Of course, this was Glasgow in wartime 'blackout', which made everything more confusing.

I followed Aunt Mary out to the street to get a tram to Great Western Road where she lived. I had never seen a tramcar, so wasn't quite sure what we were going to get into. When one came along, I thought that looks O.K. – just something like a bus (I had seen buses on the island of Skye). My only problem was that these drivers rarely came to a full stop when one wanted to get on or off. We stepped onto it quickly and, once seated, my aunt proceeded to instruct me on how to get off at our destination, without falling flat on my face. Aunt Mary said the secret was to watch as the tram slowed down, you were then to put your left foot out and step backwards, while the tram kept moving. The prospect really worried me. I was sure I would end up on my face on the street. However, it worked out fine and from then onwards, though never very confident, I coped with tramcars.

Talking of tramcars reminds me of the time my cousin Angus, Aunt Mary's son, took an old lady from

Raasay on a tramcar journey. The old lady never went anywhere without her knitting. Angus got her onto the tram and to the only available seat, near the open doorway. The old lady got out her knitting; her ball of wool fell off her lap, rolled out the door and onto the street. Angus got off and tried to retrieve it, but if you can picture a moving tram and an unwinding ball of wool, you can see he wouldn't get far. He had to chase after the wool and then catch up with the tram, especially as the old lady wouldn't know where to go or what to do.

That night, I stayed at Aunt Mary's and next morning she took me to the station to catch a train for Edinburgh. I must have shown my fear and confusion, for she went all along the platform asking likely young ladies if they were going to Dalkeith to join up. At last, she found one.

At this point, it might help you to understand my concern if I tell you what I felt. Everyone seemed to be in a hurry and I wasn't used to rushing about on my quiet little island. Time didn't mean anything there. There was no need to hurry. We had time to listen to the sound of the sea dashing against the rocks on the shore, time to listen to the sea birds calling to each other. There was time to listen to the birds singing and look for their nests in the heather and thickets. We had time to watch a beautiful sunset or sunrise – really time for everything beautiful and worthwhile. I just thought of what these people were missing, but, of course, I didn't know that life in a town is all rush and hurry.

The young lady my Aunt found going to Dalkeith was Maisie Carscadden (later Maisie Duncan) from Motherwell, and I kept in touch with her till her death a couple of years ago. We also met once since we were demobbed, when she had a holiday in the Highlands. She and her husband spent a day with me in Inverness. She was a lovely person and I was so pleased to have a train and world-wise person to keep me company. We spent our training time at Newbattle Abbey, mostly marching, 'square-bashing' and learning how to salute our superiors. At first, it seemed very strange to share life with so many girls, all sleeping in one building – not much privacy, but "we're in the Army now."

Many of the girls were from nearby towns and very used to modern life as it was then. Their outlook on life was so different from mine – all the talk was of going to the 'pictures' and dancing, while my experience of films was when I went to high school on the neighbouring island of Skye. The films were shown by a mobile film team and our cinema was the Skye Gathering hall. If I remember correctly, they only came around once a month. I don't think I saw many films, but one has really stuck in my memory. I don't remember its name; some reader probably will. I do remember it was a Charlie Chaplin film and, in it, he was so hungry he boiled his boots and proceeded to suck the nails from them with relish, as if they were juicy bones.

I only stayed in high school for a year. I was very homesick and missed my sister, Betty, who was my playmate. We were very close, just a year and a half difference in age. We must have been about the same size, for I remember we often didn't bother to see whose clothes we were putting on in the morning.

Here, far from home and all things familiar, although no longer homesick, I just felt that everyone else knew things and did things that I didn't.

It was here I met a lovely girl and a real Lady – the great, great, great grand-daughter of Sir Walter Scott. I have good reason to remember her well – because of her great kindness. I had been given the usual injections called T.A.B. I don't remember what that stood for, but I do remember how ill I became. No-one else appeared to have suffered any adverse effect, but here I was lying on my bed, feeling very miserable and far from home. Lady Patricia sympathised with me and produced some much needed aspirins. We spoke about my island roots. She showed such interest, it eased my aches and pains.

* * *

I didn't see her again till 1999. While on holiday in the borders, Hector and I visited "Abbotsford, the famous home of Sir Walter Scott. I had seen a programme on T. V. about her being the owner of Abbotsford now, but never thought I would actually meet her. I inquired from a young man at the desk and he said that she usually was about, but not today. Then someone pointed out to me her sister Lady Jean. I asked her about Patricia, and how I'd met her about 60 years before. She explained that her sister was indisposed. She had fallen the previous day and broken some ribs. She insisted that Patricia would love to see me and so it was that I met this lovely lady after so many years. We reminisced about our Dalkeith days and what had happened in our lives since then. Sadly, I read in the press a few months later that she had suddenly died. There was a great write-up about her, her charitable work and kindness to the people around – a real lady.

* * *

After our training session was over – I think it was six weeks – being A.T.S., we were asked to write on the board our preference for a posting location. I put down Gailes Camp in Ayrshire, because my sister, Peggy, was already stationed there. Maisie was fortunate. She was posted to Gailes and the Army, contrary as always, posted me to Guildford in Surrey. To me, it seemed like going to China. It was quite daunting. I just couldn't understand why Maisie went to Gailes and not me. We were both doing the same job.

However, to Guildford I had to go, and the first thing I did on arrival was to go to the A.T.S officer and apply for a posting to Gailes. In the service, an older sister could claim a younger one to join her, so Peggy duly applied. It was six months before I got my Gailes posting and believe it or not, I didn't want to go. I had made many friends at Guildford and our quarters were super. They had been pre-War married quarters and I knew that in Gailes the girls lived in Nissen huts.

Gailes was a small place outside the Ayrshire town of Irvine. I renewed my friendship with Maisie on arrival there. The Nissen huts were even worse than I had envisaged. When it rained, we had to put our waterproof gas capes over our beds. The only comforting thing was the little round coke stove in the middle of the hut. In the winter, we crowded round the warmth. Later the A.T.S. were given a beautiful golf club house to live in. (Gailes had a big golf course). This was real luxury.

I recall one night we decided it was time we did something daring. One of the office girls, Effie MacInnes, sent round little notes telling each girl what was needed.

This was it – a bundle of sticks, a candle, a bottle of soft drink and something to eat. The idea was to have a midnight feast. It was all very well but lights had to be out at 10 p.m. – hence the candles. The sticks were to kindle a fire in the huge fireplace.

Each night, a Sergeant or Corporal did Orderly Officer duty, which was to see to lights out and clock in any late passes. This night, it happened to be my sister, Peggy's, turn. As she slept upstairs, we thought she would know nothing of our activities. Unfortunately, we laughed and talked so loudly, our voices must have carried, for all of a sudden, the door opened to reveal Peggy with a look of absolute disbelief on her face, but I could just see a hint of a smile. I'm sure she struggled to keep a straight face. It was such a comic situation, a whole crowd of striped pyjama clad A.T.S. sitting round the fire by candlelight, drinking lemonade etc. I still feel like laughing when I think of think of it. By rights, we should have been put on a charge for breaking the rules, but we heard nothing more about it.

Maisie and I cooked for the Sergeants and Officers; Maisie with the Officers and I with the Sergeants. Our cookhouses were two joined Nissen huts, so we had quite a lovely time, sharing by turns for morning coffee. Some wit was heard to say that the A.T.S. cooks were Hitler's secret weapon.

Maisie was a wonderful friend. When we had free weekends, she took me to Motherwell to her parents' home. They treated me like one of the family. They had a son Andrew in the R.A.F. Sadly, his plane was brought down over Germany and he was killed.

It was in Gailes I met a girl who was to be with me for most of my days in the A.T.S. She was Chrissie McLeod from the island of Lewis. I am still in touch with her – more about Chrissie later.

My sister, Peggy, had joined up at the start of the War. She was a strict disciplinarian, but very fair. I really had to watch my Ps and Qs while stationed with her. One episode out of many comes to mind. We had to be in billets by 10 p.m., unless we had a late pass. One night, I was off duty, so visited friends from Skye who lived in Irvine. They had also invited a young man from Raasay, Murdo MacSwan and an Irish lad whom I only knew as Paddy O'Hara.

I missed the last bus to camp and, consequently, I was late. I had walked from Irvine, taking a short cut across the moor, which the lads knew of, as they were stationed in a camp somewhere on the moor. Arriving at the billets, I was met by an anxious and somewhat angry Peggy, who, pulling a watch from the pocket of her A.T.S. skirt, said, "Look at the time, my sister should show a better example."

The watch was a pocket watch that she kept on a long chain. It had belonged to my brother, John, also now in the Army. Normally, being late resulted on being put on a ‘charge’, with the resultant indignity of doing ‘jankers’ (punishment fatigues, usually the most menial jobs). However, after explaining my late appearance, I was let off the hook.

My next posting was to Hawkhead Camp near Paisley. Maisie was sent to another unit, but Chrissie and I went together to be attached to a Royal Scots unit.

From time to time, I visited my aunt in Glasgow and also my brother, James, who was married and living there. It didn’t seem so very long ago since the Glasgow traffic terrified me, but now I was finding my way about by tram and underground train around Glasgow even at night in the blackout. It still left me thinking how much more peaceful and gentle life in Eilean Tighe and Kyle Rona had been. I would never get used to noise and bustle.

Life at Hawkhead was not very exciting. I just remember one funny incident. We had a Black Watch Sergeant there who was a great piper. As I had always loved the music of the pipes, he said he would lend me a chanter. That was fine; I got the chanter and bought a pipe music book in Glasgow. Next afternoon, I sat on my bed and had a go. I don't know if you have ever heard chanter playing; it is not very sweet, even played by an expert, so you can imagine the hideous noises I produced. The girls threatened me with all sorts of punishments unless I gave up. That was the end of my piping career.

Chrissie and I decided to volunteer for service overseas. Fairly soon we were sent on embarkation leave, which meant we could go home and visit our families. My memories of the train journey north from Glasgow are very clear, but also sad. As we sat in the carriage a young soldier came in and greeted Chrissie. He was from her home village in Lewis. From his uniform, we saw he was in the Parachute Regiment. We chatted about Army life, but he seemed very concerned as to whether he would come back from this 'drop'. We knew the word meant a parachute jump, but of course, we had no idea where this 'drop' was to be.

Eventually at Kyle of Lochalsh, the end of our train journey, we boarded the R.M.S. *Lochness*, the ship to Stornoway on the Isle of Lewis, also calling to land passengers on the Isle of Raasay.

The paratrooper told me he was on seven days embarkation leave and, still seeming very much concerned about this 'drop', asked if I would come to the Raasay pier and wave to him to wish him good luck on his way back from leave. I promised to do this and was so glad afterwards that I did, because I learned from Chrissie later, when she had a letter from her mother in Lewis, telling her that the young man was killed at the battle of Arnhem – the 'drop' that he had been so concerned about. What a tragedy it turned out to be for many young paratroopers.

When Chrissie and I returned from leave, we were posted to a transit camp at Bristol to await orders for overseas. If I remember right, we were at Bristol for three or four days before being sent to Southend, where next morning, we were to board a ship for the Continent. That night, I heard and saw something that was really frightening – German V1 flying bombs. We heard their dreadful droning noise, followed by an ominous silence as the engine cut out. You knew it was then going to come down and cause dreadful havoc.

Later that evening, we boarded ship, along with two other A.T.S girls. We were handed two items, a bag for sickness and a red light to clip to our battledress tunics, so that, if the ship was torpedoed, rescuers would be able to see us in the water. That night we slept on board, an unforgettable experience, my first and last time in a hammock.

My first sight of the other side was very sobering; near the shore, as far as the eye could see, were many sunken ships, half submerged and lying at grotesque angles, some with sterns or stems still above the surface. It really was a most disturbing sight and something that has remained with me to this day. Our destination had been Ostend, where our arrival was greeted with wolf whistles from soldiers billeted in the nearby buildings.

Following a meal, we were taken to Lille in France, where, after another meal, we spent the night. We were glad of a rest, although the other three girls decided to see the town. I settled for an early night. Our sleeping quarters were in the attic of an old building with exposed rafters. My eye caught sight of a newspaper pushed behind one of these and I thought – no good trying to read that, it will be in French. Imagine my surprise when I unfolded it to read '*The Islay Gazette*', Islay of course being another of our Scottish islands. To me, it was like finding a piece of home. I spent the evening reading months old news of Islay. Some Scottish soldier had slept there before us.

In the morning, we were off again in an Army truck, this time to Amiens, our destination the 121st British General Hospital. We were ordered to report to a Captain Wiggington, a kind, likeable chap who handed us, most importantly, Red Cross cards, so that, if we were taken prisoner, we would be treated as Red Cross personnel.

Also, from somewhere for each of us, he produced talcum powder, perfume, bath salts, all beautiful French make, and a wallet with small notebook that I have till this day.

We were sent to the hospital kitchen straight away. There, all the cooks were A.C.C. (Army Catering Corps), with some French civilian women as helpers. We could immediately feel the animosity from these ladies, as up till then, the men were all theirs. We got some sour looks and certainly not welcoming ones.

Our first job from the Corporal Cook in Charge was scrubbing the very dirty floor. It was quite a big room and we thought the floor was concrete. It was really caked with cookhouse grease and mud. The A.C.C. cooks thought it wasn't their job, they were there to cook. They left it to the French women, who never cleaned it, as we found out when we tried mopping it with hot soapy water – no effect at all. With much murmuring, we got down on our knees with scrubbing brushes. Lo and behold, our labours revealed beautiful black and white tiles, a great surprise for us and seemingly for the men cooks, or so they said.

It was here in Amiens that I met my future husband Arthur. He was a special diet cook, catering for men with bad stomachs, usually through being wounded. I didn't really get to know him till later when we moved our hospital into Germany.

The complete 121st B.G.H. moved into Germany. That was to be a memorable journey. We were heading for Celle, a town in Lower Saxony in Germany. The War had not yet ended, but getting close to it. There was utter confusion on the roads. Travelling in convoy, for some reason our truck became separated from the others. We were oblivious to the fact till we heard the noise of German heavy artillery. It was quite hair-raising. We all got out our Red Cross cards, but thankfully, they weren't needed. Our driver, realising his mistake, managed to rejoin the convoy. We all heaved a sigh of relief.

We stopped for a few days at a place called Hassalt in Belgium. We were billeted in a deserted farmhouse; I don't know where the inhabitants had gone. It was quite deserted, but obviously, someone must have been coming to the farm to tend the animals, or else the farm people had not long gone.

Chrissie and I wandered round looking for a private spot to answer the call of nature, when we heard the unmistakable sound of a cow being milked; it sounded a contented cow too. We peeped round the corner into the stall where a cow was tied up. Instead of being milked by the farmer, happily milking away was Paddy one of our cooks skilfully performing that duty. He thought we could do with some fresh milk and we did. We also found the necessary private place, a pigsty, fortunately minus pigs.

Next stop was at a place called Heek on the Dutch-German border, where we stayed one night – then on into Germany. We four girls had the distinction of being the first A.T.S. to cross the Rhine, en route for Celle, where we took over a former German gas training school as the new 121st B.G.H.

During our long journey from France, I was appalled at the carnage I saw. Most vividly in my memory are the many graves by the roadside, identified by hurriedly improvised wooden crosses, often topped with an Allied or German helmet. It brought home to me the terrible waste of young lives and the fact that underneath these crosses were men who were someone's loved ones. Up till then, the killing didn't seem so real. One read about it, or heard it on the radio, but here was the reality. Something else that made a great impression on me were the many dead animals, cows and horses, their grotesque bodies bloated by the heat of the summer sun. These poor animals had wandered into the mined fields. I think my outrage at seeing these poor dumb animals was increased by having always being involved with animals on my father's croft in Raasay.

There were signs of fierce fighting everywhere along the road. Most villages through which we passed had the house walls pitted by mortar and cannon fire. As we travelled, we met German prisoners being marched along with their hands up. They looked a pathetic lot; many of them were little more than boys; one couldn't help feeling sorry for them.

* * *

There was one incident that makes me smile even now – it was the amusing sight of a British soldier sitting on top of a tank plucking a chicken. We all cheered him as we passed. After the sad sights we had witnessed, it was good to be able to laugh; most of the time, one felt more like crying.

In Celle, we were pleased to find beautiful living quarters and even a swimming pool. For some reason, we didn't use the kitchen. Perhaps the previous occupants had seen to it that it was unusable. Whatever the reason, we had to improvise a hut that served as a kitchen. The men set to and built a wooden shack, open fronted, no windows and no doors. Fortunately, it was a warm summer. Our primitive cooker consisted of some metal sheets with a fire underneath, fuelled from a pipe dripping fuel oil onto it – it served the purpose.

After about a week, we were able to use the barrack kitchen, which was wonderful; it had all the electric equipment you could think of. We were not many days in Celle when some of the boys brought us rolls of the most beautiful German parachute silk. It was of much finer and better quality than the British equivalent. Before leaving Celle, I had my wedding dress, a lovely creation made from it by a German dressmaker. I found that all the German women, young or old, were good at dressmaking and other handicrafts. I don't suppose many brides have been married in a German parachute.

By the time we arrived in Celle, the War in Europe had ended and we were given German civilians to help us. At times, it was quite amusing – there was a 'no fraternisation' order in force. Can you imagine working with someone with whom you had no quarrel and staying silent? When the Officers and NCOs were not around, the order was ignored.

One unusual and amusing incident occurred when Molly, our Irish member, and I were sitting in the sun, peeling potatoes. A German officer in full uniform came along and stood looking at us. We had often seen this man marching prisoners to duties in various parts of the hospital. It got Molly's 'Irish' up to see him standing there and we two working. She shouted at him, "What are you staring at? It would be better if you helped, but you wouldn't know how to peel a potato."

He asked for a knife and proceeded very skilfully to peel potatoes. There was silence for a while and then he asked in perfect English, "Are you English?" Of course, we quickly advised him "We are Irish and Scottish". I enlarged upon it by saying I came from the Highlands of Scotland, whereupon our German 'guest', in perfect English, gave us a rendering of the song "*My heart's in the Highlands, my heart is not here*". I asked him where he had learned English and heard that song. He told me it was during his time at Oxford University. He made a good job of peeling spuds and put Irish Molly firmly in her place.

My stay in Celle had one very sad incident that took place on VE (Victory in Europe) celebration night. We had a special dinner put on, which we enjoyed, as the girls didn't have to do anything. The men did the catering and we had a most enjoyable time, which unfortunately ended in tragedy. After dinner that lasted till nearly midnight, a midnight swim was suggested and several of us did. We didn't swim (I couldn't) and we just sat at the poolside. Later, we realised one of the men was missing – Johnny Johnson. At first, we thought he was just playing the fool, perhaps hiding in the nearby bushes, but then after calling him and searching, we came to the awful conclusion that he had not come out of the pool. It was a terrible moment when we realised that Johnny was in there while we wasted time looking for him. The men swam underwater looking for him, but to no avail. The Orderly Officer was called and he ordered the pool to be drained. Pumps were brought and by the lights of trucks, draining commenced. We girls were sent to our billets, which overlooked the pool. The men said they would tell us when Johnny was found. We waited at one of the open windows till one of them shouted up that they had found poor Johnny's body. It was really a terrible end to a happy evening. Johnny worked with us girls and was always the life and soul of the party, a really lovely fellow.

It was more tragic that he had come through all the fighting in the East and France, and then to die on Victory night. We were even more saddened when we learned that Johnny had a young wife and baby. I realise now, since becoming a Christian, that each day is in God's hands. We cannot live longer or die sooner than He decrees.

Celle is very near the notorious Belsen Bergen concentration camp, so when some of the R.A.S.C. boys stationed with us and who often went there with supplies, asked if we would like to go there, we readily agreed, but didn't dream of what we were to see.

Belsen had been liberated about a fortnight when we visited it. It was a truly awesome experience. Because of typhus fever, we were not allowed to alight from the truck. There were notices everywhere warning of typhus, so we drove slowly through. We had already seen some of the victims, as our hospital had an intake of some 'able to walk' ones and poor souls who, following the deprivations, were unable to eat ordinary food. Nothing could prepare us for what we saw that day. Sitting outside long huts were people who really didn't look alive. There bodies had no flesh and even the bones looked as if they had shrunk. There were notices on the doors detailing the deaths that day and from the look of those sitting there, they would probably soon be on the list too. Those we saw were the fitter ones. The worse cases were in No.12 B.G.H. that was now situated in Belsen.

Just one thought came to mind. It didn't seem possible to me that any human being could inflict such devilish cruelty upon another. It was a sight, which, as I write nearly sixty years on, I can still vividly see before my eyes. One can only imagine the scenes of horror that met the liberating troops when they first entered these huts. I have read since that the first soldiers to enter came out quickly and were immediately sick. Here was 'man's inhumanity to man' on a 'never before' scale.

Following our time in Celle, the 121st B.G.H moved to Brunswick in the same region of Germany. There, we took over the former headquarters of German Field-marshal Karl von Rundstedt. Someone must have left in a hurry; there was a half eaten meal still on the table. It was a beautiful building and very well furnished. The kitchen was even superior to the one at Celle. The main building had its own cinema and underground hospital, fully equipped with a modern operating theatre. The Quartermaster's stores were also underground and here my A.T.S. friends and I had a field-day. There were all kinds of Officer's equipment and uniforms, and caps with wonderful colourful badges. We helped ourselves to souvenirs. Molly even took an Officer's complete uniform, including some kind of revolver. Later that evening, she dressed up as a Gestapo officer. She really looked the part, but her Irish accent gave her away.

It was while we were at Brunswick that Arthur and I really got to know each other, although we had a couple of walks out at Celle. From here, we went home on leave, saw Arthur's parents and were engaged. Our time together was soon cut short when the powers that be decided to post Arthur to Lunenburg, and shortly after, all the A.T.S were told that we were to be posted to different units. At Brunswick, Chrissie Macleod also met her future husband and was married there, given away by our Officer Commanding, Colonel Day. Irish Molly met her future husband in the hospital and our fourth member, Betty, was courting a Medical Orderly. I don't know if that became permanent or not, as I lost touch with her after Brunswick. While I was there, I had the great pleasure of seeing Field-Marshal Montgomery. He was inspecting troops at nearby Fallingbostel. Some army trucks were going there, so Chrissie and I decided we couldn't miss the opportunity of seeing this great man.

Thus, we four parted company. It was inevitable, as we were heading for our 'demob' dates. Ironically, Arthur had been posted back to the hospital just a few days before I left. I was sent to Iserlohn near Dortmund and, as soon as I was able to get a weekend pass, I headed for Brunswick. But easier said than done. I intended catching a Services' (Army) train that ran at certain times, but, by the time I got off duty and reached the station, they had stopped running for the day. Here I was, in a strange foreign railway station, with displaced persons milling about everywhere, even sitting on the roof of a train that had just pulled in.

Out of the corner of my eye, I saw a Redcap (Military Police) looking my way. Oh dear, what now? I was O.K.

as far as being out of camp was concerned, but I was only allowed to travel by Services' train. Well, I wasn't going to worry – "He may be just looking for improperly dressed soldiers, or even deserters." I pretended not to see him, but he definitely saw me and he was coming towards me. He asked where I was intending travelling. I said, "To Brunswick," to which he replied, "There are no Service trains to Brunswick or anywhere near it tonight." He saw me looking towards the train standing there, and with, "O.K., I haven't seen you," he turned and walked away. I had told him why I was going to Brunswick, so I think he was a bit of a romantic.

I quickly got on the train; the seats were all wooden slatted, not made for comfort! It was packed with civilians, mostly displaced persons. No one was making much conversation, but maybe they were different nationalities. I wondered if I had been wise. It looked as if I was the only Service person on the train, certainly in that carriage. However, I had got this far and I knew that, if I could get to Hanover station, there was an A.T.S. holding unit there.

I reached Hanover without incident and phoned our A.T.S unit to ask for transport. That was the normal routine, but obviously not at that time of night. The Duty Officer who answered my call could not grasp how I got there, as there were no Service trains in the evening. After some time trying to convince her, she turned quite severe and ordered me to report to her office. She would send transport for me but "that was not condoning what I did." This sounded bad. It looked as if I was for a 'charge', and that would mean going before the Commanding Officer and taking whatever punishment she meted out, usually 'confined to barracks' for a period.

The transport duly turned up and, on arrival at the unit, I reported at the office as ordered. The officer there listened to my story about travelling on a civilian train and said, "You know that is a serious punishable offence."

Perhaps I looked very contrite, or maybe more like a displaced person myself, for she was sympathetic and asked where I was going to stay in Brunswick, as all the A.T.S. personnel had left. I, of course, knew this and told her I planned to stay with the V.A.D. (Voluntary Aid Detachment) hospital nurses. What I didn't know was that the V.A.D.s had already moved on.

I got an army truck from Hanover to somewhere outside Brunswick. The driver deposited me outside a big building with a sentry on guard. I never found out what place it was. I walked up to the guard and told him where I wanted to go. He was a real answer to my prayer. He stopped a passing truck and asked the driver to take me to the 121st B.G.H. To say I was relieved was to put it mildly. However, my troubles were not quite over. As I mentioned earlier the V.A.D.s had gone. Arthur consulted his Commanding Officer, who must have been from a different mould to some I had known. He asked to speak to me and very kindly said, if I didn't mind, I could sleep in one of the wards as long as the patients didn't know. It was hilarious. When bedtime came, the Ward Orderly who was in on the secret, put screens round my bed, which was conveniently near the door so no one saw me come in or go out. I expect the patients thought I was a dying companion, or had a contagious disease.

Altogether, it was quite an adventure, one that in my wildest dreams, I wouldn't have imagined in my young days in Kyle Rona. The whole thing went off very well. I returned to Iserlohn in the authorised Services' train. Thereafter, my stay there was uneventful.

Billeted in a comfortable German house at Iserlohn, my A.T.S. days were at last coming to an end. I felt a bit sad, but I was looking forward to getting home again.

In due time, I returned to Britain and was demobbed at York. That was where we actually signed ourselves out of active service, handed in our kit and received our 'gratuity' money. This was intended to help us buy civilian clothes. There was about enough for a coat and shoes.

The train heading north for Glasgow seemed even slower than usual. Maybe I was just growing impatient for that first glimpse of Dun Cann, a landmark mountain on Raasay, and believed to be an extinct volcano. Dun Cann told me I was near home, always a welcome sight and it still is. I was never so pleased to see it, as after the long journey from Iserlohn to Raasay.

Before leaving Germany, Arthur and I had decided we would marry when he was demobbed, which came a few months after I left for home.

My stay at home in Raasay did not last long. Arthur's hometown was Beccles in Suffolk. At first, I had great difficulty understanding the Suffolk dialect, especially the older people like Arthur's mum and dad. They also had their problems with my Hebridean accent. For some time, Arthur had to act as interpreter. An occasion comes to mind when I think of language difficulty.

One day, when I went into a shop in Beccles and asked for a comb, the assistant looked blankly at me and said, "I don't think we have any." I had to demonstrate the use of a comb, whereupon she said, "Ow, you mean a cowm."

Our 'o' is very broad and much different from the English one.

* * *

In time, I became used to things and grew quite fond of Beccles and its people, whom I found friendly and helpful. My two daughters, Heather and Rona, were born in Beccles and I lived there for seventeen years, before moving to a small Norfolk village called Poringland. This was because of a change in Arthur's work scene. Sadly, he died there in 1978 at the age of fifty-eight.

Afterwards, I moved for a time to Mattishall, another Norfolk village, where I found pleasant and helpful friends. Here, I mention especially the Bash family. However, I always longed to return to Scotland. I missed the hills and the islands. When my daughters were both married and with their own families, I decided it was time to move back to my roots. I had lived in England for forty years, but never forgot my native Gaelic tongue. I often found myself thinking in Gaelic while speaking in English. I sold up and bought a house in Inverness. I also bought an old caravan, which the Bash sons, Andrew and Timothy, towed all the way from Norfolk to Raasay.

That was quite a feat. It had to be taken across two small ferries; we didn't have the Skye Bridge at that time.

I spent a lot of time in that old caravan in the next two years, even a cold two months one winter. While there one Christmas, I saw an unusual sight. My elder brother, John, a bachelor who lived alone, had allowed me to site my caravan in his garden. One very cold morning, everything covered in snow, I took John (still in bed) a cup of tea. To my amazement, sitting on his bedpost, was a robin, quite unafraid.

"John," I called, "there's a bird on your bedpost."

"Oh, that's O.K.," he said "that's Robbie. He comes in every morning."

A few years after coming to Inverness, I met Hector, my present husband. He has been very patient with me, spending so much time writing and helping with typing. Hector and I have a very special thing in common. We are both professing Christians, which makes for a very happy married life. My daughters, between them, have given me four grandsons and now one of these, Geoffrey and his wife Mina, have presented me in these last few years with two dear little great grand-daughters, Emma and Jenifer. The Lord has been good to me.

I appreciate all the convenience modern living has brought me, but on the whole, this generation are less contented and less caring. I feel very sorry for the majority of young folk today. They seem to have everything modern that money can buy, but they will never know the peace and contentment I enjoyed while growing up in Eilean Tighe and Kyle Rona.

Me c.1942

Sister Peggy and Me at Gailes Camp, 1942

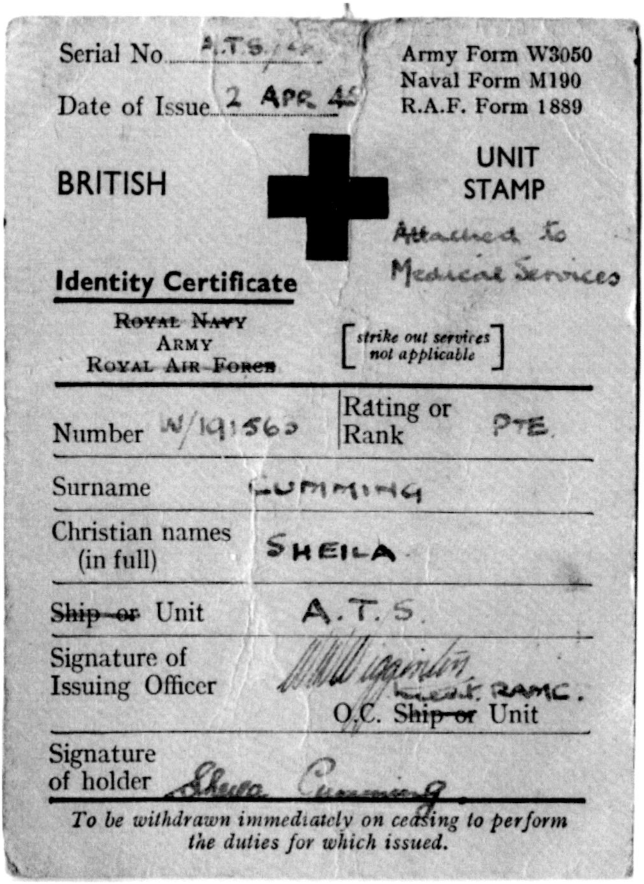

Serial No. A.T.S./..

Date of Issue 2 APR 45

Army Form W3050
Naval Form M190
R.A.F. Form 1889

BRITISH

UNIT STAMP

Attached to Medical Services

Identity Certificate

~~Royal Navy~~
Army
~~Royal Air Force~~

[strike out services not applicable]

Number W/191560	Rating or Rank PTE.

Surname CUMMING

Christian names (in full) SHEILA.

~~Ship or~~ Unit A.T.S.

Signature of Issuing Officer [signature] ~~Lieut.~~ RAMC.
O.C. ~~Ship or~~ Unit

Signature of holder Sheila Cumming

To be withdrawn immediately on ceasing to perform the duties for which issued.

My Red Cross card

Sheila is Gaelic for Julia

The former German Army gas school at Celle

The German gas school with Red Cross on roof,
hopefully to prevent us being bombed. In the foreground is the swimming pool where Johnny Johnson so tragically drowned

We four, the first A.T.S. to cross the Rhine – Me, Chrissie Macleod, Betty, and "Irish" Molly Maclung at Celle.

The improvised cookhouse at Celle – Me and one of the lads

Johnny Johnson's grave in the War Cemetery at Celle,
A sad reminder of the terrible cost of War

Maisie Duncan, née Carscadden, and me in 1989

Reunion after 47 years

My first marriage – Arthur and I
Sister Betty, bridesmaid, seated on right, Arthur's parents, extreme right

My second marriage, Hector and I – 1991

My daughters Heather and Rona
at age 3½ years and 6 months

Raasay shearing—John, a neighbour, Callum Ban, me and my faithful dog, Tammy

Brother John at shearing